100% COTTON YARN

HELLO

T0290300

HELLO
Amigurumi

HAPPY CHILDHOOD DAYS

Damla SAVAŞ
Dilek BİRKAN
Elisa EMS-DOMENIG
Gülizar SEZER
Kate&Dasha
Mei LI LEE
Sandra MULLER
Skaiste KIVCI
Vivyane VEKA

100% COTTON YARN

Tuva

Tuva Publishing
www.tuvapublishing.com

Address Merkez Mah. Cavusbasi Cad. No71
Cekmekoy - Istanbul 34782 / Turkey
Tel +9 0216 642 62 62

HELLO Amigurumi

First Print 2022 / March

All Global Copyrights Belong To
Tuva Tekstil ve Yayıncılık Ltd.

Content Crochet

Editor in Chief Ayhan DEMİRPEHLİVAN

Project Editor Kader DEMİRPEHLİVAN

Designers Damla SAVAŞ, Dilek BİRKAN, Elisa EMS-DOMENIG,
Gülizar SEZER, Kate&Dasha, Mei LI LEE, Sandra MULLER,
Skaiste KIVCI, Vivyane VEKA

Technical Editor Leyla ARAS

Graphic Designers Ömer ALP, Abdullah BAYRAKÇI, Tarık TOKGÖZ

Photography Tuva Publishing

Crochet Tech Editor Wendi CUSINS

All rights are reserved. No part of this publication may be
reproduced, stored in a retrieval system, or transmitted
in any form or by any means, electronic, mechanical,
photocopying, recording, or otherwise, without prior
written consent of the publisher. The copyrights of the
designs in this book are protected and may not be used
for any commercial purpose.

ISBN 978-605-7834-54-6

 TuvaYayincilik    TuvaPublishing

 TuvaYayincilik    TuvaPublishing

Introduction

Welcome to the world of amigurumi! This is where you can go back to happy childhood days with lovely amigurumi dolls and toys.

This wonderful collection of nineteen original crochet designs takes you on a journey of happy childhood memories. You will discover some beginner-friendly patterns as well as more advanced designs (if you're up for a challenge!), making this book suitable for all crochet skill levels.

With each project you will find easy to follow crochet instructions, supported by step-by-step clear photographs. The special stitches and techniques used in the designs are fully explained to help you on your amigurumi journey.

We are grateful to the nine talented and accomplished amigurumi designers (from all over the world) who contributed to this book. They each bring their own characteristic flair and style to their beautiful designs.

Among this wonderful collection of toys, we are sure you'll find something to make and treasure. Whether you are crocheting these handmade toys as a gift or even for yourself, you will be creating everlasting memories.

Happy Crocheting!

TUVA

STACY SPORTY AND SWEET
P. 24

FLYNN AND ABBY
THE BABY DOLL TWINS
P. 36

MAYA THE BUNNY
P. 44

COWGIRL
P. 52

CANDICE
P. 62

MATILDA
P. 70

EMILY THE GARDENER
P. 78

GRANDMA AND GRANDPA
P. 86

GRANNY AND HER LITTLE HELPER
P. 96

LITTLE BUNNY
P. 110

LITTLE SUZIE
P. 116

AUDREY
P. 124

RILEY THE RAG DOLL
P.134

ROBOT BOY
P.141

HARLEY THE DUCKLING
P.149

WINTER BEAR
P.154

CONTENTS

Introduction - 3

Materials We Used - 8

General Information for Making Amigurumi - 12

Adapting The Design - 13

Crochet Terminology - 13

Crochet Basics - 14

Special Stitches Used in Amigurumi - 16

Crochet Techniques For Amigurumi - 17

Jointed Toys - 18

Embriodery Stitches - 19

Assembling Amigurumi Pieces Together - 20

PROJECTS

Stacy Sporty and Sweet - 24

Flynn and Abby The Baby Doll Twins - 36

Maya The Bunny - 44

Cowgirl - 52

Candice - 62

Matilda - 70

Emily The Gardener - 78

Grandma and Grandpa - 86

Granny and Her Little Helper - 96

Little Bunny - 110

Little Suzie - 116

Audrey - 124

Riley The Rag Doll - 134

Robot Boy - 141

Harley The Duckling - 149

Winter Bear - 154

Materials
&
Tools

Crochet
&
Amigurumi
Basics

Materials We Used

Safety Warning

When making toys for children under the age of three (including babies), be sure to use child-friendly products.

We advise you avoid the following:

• 'Fuzzy' yarns, where the lint can be inhaled or swallowed.
• Glass Eyes or beads, which can shatter or break.
• Small beads and buttons (including some safety eyes) can be chewed off and swallowed or become a choking hazard.

General Safety Tips

1 Make sure each piece of the toy is sewn firmly onto the body.

2 Instead of using Safety Eyes, buttons or beads, you can use crocheted or felt circles, sewn on firmly.

3 You can create features on your toys with simple embroidery stitches.

Note: These Safety Warnings also apply when you make toys for pets.

The Yarns

All the designs in this book were made using the HELLO Cotton Yarn. We prefer using the cotton yarns when making toys. It is a natural fiber and easy to care for, as it is machine-washable.

If you want to substitute the yarns used in the patterns with other yarn, please adjust your hook size to get either the correct gauge or 'feel' of the fabric.

The Hooks

We love using the Clover Amour Hooks which are ergonomic, comfortable and easy to hold. Each size hook has its own color, making it easy to remember which hook you're using.

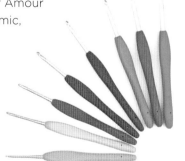

Hook Size Conversion Table

Metric	U.S.	UK/Canada
2.25 mm	B-1	13
2.75 mm	C-2	12
3.00 mm	-	11
3.25 mm	D-3	10
3.50 mm	E-4	-
3.75 mm	F-5	9
4.00 mm	G-6	8
4.50 mm	7	7
5.00 mm	H-8	6
5.50 mm	I-9	5
6.00 mm	J-10	4
6.50 mm	K-10 ½	3

The Stuffing

When it comes to stuffing your toys, there are quite a few options available. Whichever stuffing you choose, make sure it is fluffy and does not clump. We used **polyester fiberfill** (also known as polyfill or fiberfill) for the stuffing in all the toys.

Polyester pellets (which are heavier than stuffing) can also be used if you want a bit of weight in your toy. You can also combine polyfill with pellets while stuffing.

Please do NOT use stuffing like rice or beans, which might rot and decay, which could attract creepy crawlies.

HELLO
76 COLOURS

ART.C25
+/- 25G - 62.5M - 68YDS
76 COLOURS

ART.C50
+/- 50G - 125M - 136YDS
76 COLOURS

3
10x10cm / 4"x4"
2.5 - 3.5

10x10cm / 4"x4"
2.5
27
24

N 161	114	125	137	153
N 162	115	126	138	154
N 163	116	127	139	155
101	117	128	140	156
102	118	129	141	N 173
103	119	130	142	157
104	120	N 169	143	158
105	121	N 170	144	N 174
106	122	131	145	159
107	123	133	146	N 175
108	N 164	134	147	N 176
109	124	132	148	160
110	N 165	N 171	149	
111	N 166	135	150	
112	N 167	136	151	
113	N 168	N 172	152	

CONFIDENCE IN TEXTILES
Tested for harmful substances
according to Oeko-Tex Standard 100
15 HTR 73292   HOHENSTEIN HTTI

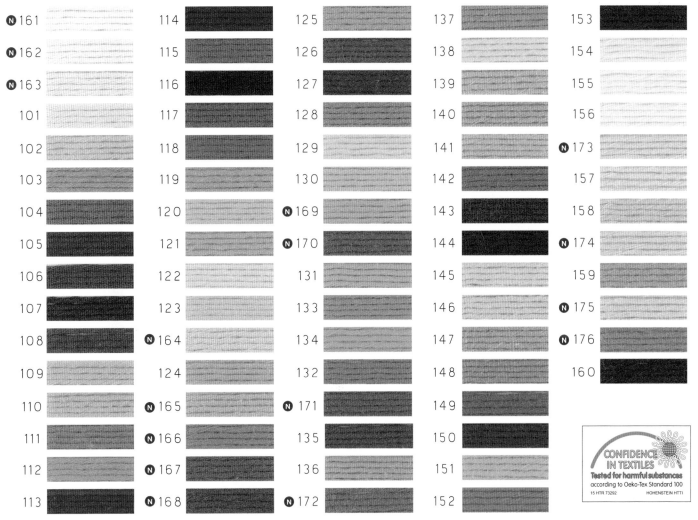

9

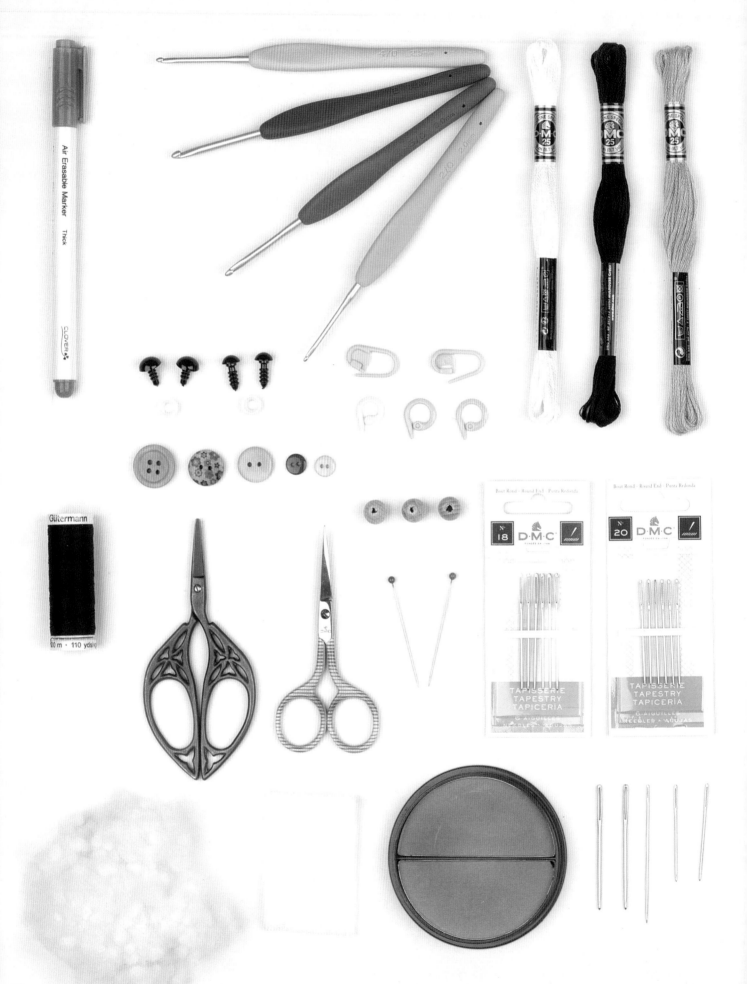

The Stitch Markers

Keeping track of the last (or first) stitch while working a crocheted spiral round is important for the stitch counts. Locking stitch markers are the best tool for this as they can be opened and closed easily.

Alternatively, you can use a separate piece of yarn (in another color), a safety pin, or even a paperclip.

The Yarn (Tapestry) Needle

This needle is needed for joining the different crochet pieces together, as well as for weaving in the yarn ends.

Preferably use a blunt-tipped needle which will not split the yarn. You could also use a bent-tip tapestry needle. Make sure the eye of the needle is large enough for the yarn you're using. We also find that the metal needles work much better with amigurumi than the plastic needles.

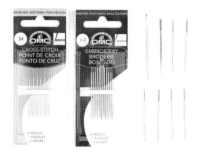

The Safety Eyes (& Noses)

Eyes and facial features give the toys character. Using safety eyes and a safety nose is a quick way of achieving this. Generally the eye or nose is attached to a ribbed shank, which is inserted through the fabric. A locking washer is applied to the shank, keeping the eye (or nose) in place. These eyes and noses can be made from plastic, glass or acrylic, and come in a range of shapes, sizes and colors. Once they are attached, it is almost impossible to pull them out. Before using them, please read the Safety Warning.

Sometimes it is easy enough to attach these eyes using only your fingers. For those who find it difficult, there is a safety eye insertion tool which can be used to attach the washers.

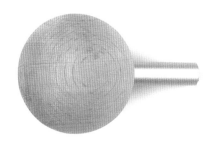

The Embroidery Floss / Perle Cotton Thread

DMC has wide range of Perle or Stranded cottons, which can be used to embellish your toys. You can use them to embroider facial features, or enhance their overall appearance by adding cross-stitch motifs or embroidered flowers.

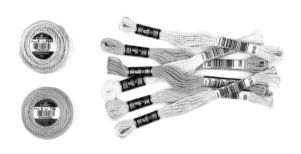

The Felts & Fabrics

Using small pieces of felt or fabric is also a great way to embellish your toys. They can be used as appliqué patches or as clothing accessories, like scarves.

The Sewing Needle & Thread

When we need to apply appliqué (either crocheted of fabric), we use a needle and thread. Use a good quality thread to sew the pieces on securely.

The Other Materials

Small Scissors

Straight Pins (with large heads)

Pompom makers

Buttons

Cosmetic blusher for cheeks

General Information for Making Amigurumi

Choosing the Hook

Use a hook which is a size or two smaller than what is recommended on the yarn label. The fabric created should be tight enough so that the stuffing does not show through the stitches.

Right Side vs Wrong Side of the Fabric

It is important to be able to distinguish between the 'right' (front) and 'wrong' (back) side of the crocheted fabric.

Right Side

Wrong Side

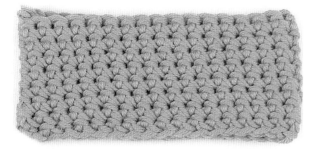

When working in a spiral or joined round, the right side of the fabric is always facing you. Working in rows or turned rounds, it will alternate between 'right' and 'wrong' side.

Single Crochet Rows

Working in a Spiral

Most of the amigurumi pieces are worked in a continuous spiral to create the dimensional shapes needed. Working in a spiral means that at the end of a round, you do not join (or close) with a slip stitch into the first stitch of the round. When you get to the end of the round, you start the next round by just working a stitch into the next stitch (which is the first stitch of the previous round).

Using Stitch Markers

When working in a spiral, it is important to keep track of the round you are working on as well as the stitch count for the round. To do this, use a stitch marker placed in the last stitch of the round. Some people prefer marking the first stitch of the round. Whichever you choose, keep consistent throughout project piece.

Hint Count your stitches after each round (and row) to ensure you have the correct stitch count.

Working in Joined (Closed) Rounds

Some parts of an amigurumi pattern might have 'joined rounds'. This is where, at the end of the round, you join with a slip stitch in the first stitch of the round. The next round starts with a number of chain stitches (based on height of the stitches used), and then you continue working stitches for the next round.

Note Do not turn at the end of each joined round, unless instructed to do so.

Working in Rows

For some accessories or patches for your amigurumi, you will need to work in rows. Each row starts by turning the piece and working some chain stitches (known as the 'turning chain'). The number of chain stitches worked is based on the height of the stitches used.

Stuffing

The pieces of the toys need to get stuffed to hold their correct shape. Some pieces only need a "light stuffing" – just enough stuffing to hold the shape. When the pattern calls for a piece to be "stuffed firmly", you need to stuff it as tight as you can, and then add a bit more. The back of your crochet hook or a plastic chopstick can be used as a stuffing tool to help you spread the stuffing into every little nook and cranny.

Tip Stuff the pieces of your toy as you're making them.

Adapting The Design

There are many ways you can make your amigurumi toy unique.

Size By choosing a different weight yarn, you can make your toys either bigger (using thicker yarn) or smaller (using thinner yarn or thread). Remember to change your hook size too.

Colors This is the easiest way to make your toy unique. Select colors to match décor or personal preference

Characteristics Changing the facial features of toys, gives them a whole new character. By adding (or removing) embellishments to the overall toy, can change the whole look of it.

Eyes Just by changing the size or color of the eyes, can create a totally different facial expression. Instead of using safety eyes, you can use buttons or beads for eyes. If there is a safety concern, you can sew on small bits of felt for eyes or embroider the features.

Blusher Adding some color to the cheeks, is another way of changing the character of toys. You can apply cosmetic pink blusher or eyeshadow using a small makeup brush or cotton bud (Q-Tip). Another way to do this, is to rub a red pencil on a piece of fabric, pressing down hard. Then rub the 'red' fabric on the cheeks as blusher.

Applique patches Whether they are crocheted, fabric or felt (or a combination of these), adding appliqué patches to your doll is a great way to make your toys distinctive. They can be facial features, such as eyes, noses, mouths, cheeks, and maybe even ears. You can also make novelty appliqué patches to use as embellishment on the toys. For example – flowers on a dress, eye-patch for a pirate, overall patch for a farmer. The creativity becomes endless.

Embroidery By adding embroidery stitches to the face, the character of the toy can change. Whether you use plain embroidery stitches (straight stitch, back stitch, etc.) or fancy ones (satin stitch, French knot, bullion stitch, etc.), your toy will take on a personality of its own. You can also use the cross-stitch technique to create a unique look.

Note Embroider all facial features to make a child-safe toy.

Crochet surface stitches This technique is worked on a finished crochet fabric. It can be used for outlines, emphasis or decoration.

Pompoms These little balls are very versatile. Making them in different sizes, you can use them as bunny tails, or to decorate the toy. A great tool to use is the Clover pompom maker, which comes in various sizes. You can also make them using other methods, like wrapping around a fork or piece of cardboard.

Adding Accessories To create your one-of-a-kind toy, you can add various decorations to them. Colored buttons can be used in a variety of ways to spice things up. Using small ribbons and bows can feminize dolls. Attaching a small bunch of flowers or small basket to a doll's hand, tells a new story.

However you choose to give your toy character, each one ends up being unique!

Crochet Terminology

This book uses US crochet terminology.

Basic conversion chart

US	UK
slip stitch **(sl st)**	slip stitch **(sl st)**
chain **(ch)**	chain **(ch)**
single crochet **(sc)**	double crochet **(dc)**
double crochet **(dc)**	treble crochet **(tr)**
half-double crochet **(hdc)**	half treble **(htr)**
treble (triple) crochet **(tr)**	double treble **(dtr)**

Abbreviations Of The Basic Stitches

ch	Chain Stitch
sl st	Slip Stitch
sc	Single Crochet Stitch
hdc	Half-Double Crochet Stitch
dc	Double Crochet Stitch
tr	Treble (or Triple) Crochet Stitch

Concise Action Terms

dec	Decrease (reduce by one or more stitches)
inc	Increase (add one or more stitches)
join	Join two stitches together, usually with a slip stitch. (Either to complete the end of a round or when introducing a new ball or color of yarn)
rep	Repeat (the previous marked instructions)
turn	Turn your crochet piece so you can work back for the next row/round
yo	Yarn over the hook. (Either to pull up a loop or to draw through the loops on hook)

Standard Symbols Used in Patterns

[ ]	Work instructions within brackets as many times as directed
( )	Work instructions within parentheses in same stitch or space indicated
*	Repeat the instructions following the single asterisk as directed
**	1) Repeat instructions between asterisks as many times as directed; or 2) Repeat from a given set of instructions

Crochet Basics

Slip Knot

Almost every crochet project starts with a slip knot on the hook. This is not mentioned in any pattern – it is assumed.

To make a slip knot, form a loop with your yarn (the tail end hanging behind your loop); insert the hook through the loop, and pick up the ball end of the yarn. Draw yarn through loop. Keeping loop on hook, gently tug the tail end to tighten the knot. Tugging the ball end tightens the loop.

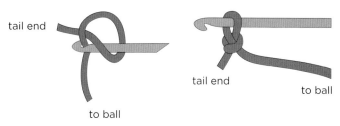

tail end

to ball

tail end

to ball

Yarn Over (yo)

This is a common practice, especially with the taller stitches. With a loop on your hook, wrap the yarn (attached to the ball) from back to front around the shaft of your hook.

Chain Stitch (ch)

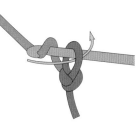

The chain stitch is the foundation of most crochet projects. The foundation chain is a series of chain stitches in which you work the first row of stitches.

To make a chain stitch, you start with a slip knot (or loop) on the hook. Yarn over and pull the yarn through the loop on your hook (first chain stitch made). For more chain stitches, repeat: Yarn over, pull through loop on hook.

Hint Don't pull the stitches too tight, otherwise they will be difficult to work in. When counting chain stitches, do not count the slip knot, nor the loop on the hook. Only count the number of 'v's.

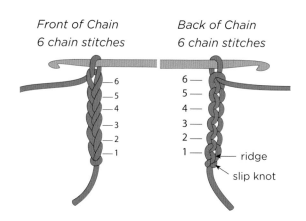

Front of Chain
6 chain stitches

Back of Chain
6 chain stitches

6
5
4
3
2
1

6
5
4
3
2
1

ridge

slip knot

Slip Stitch (sl st)

Starting with a loop on your hook, insert hook in stitch or space specified and pull up a loop, pulling it through the loop on your hook as well.

The slip stitch is commonly used to attach new yarn and to join rounds.

Attaching a New Color or New Ball of Yarn or Joining with a Slip Stitch (join with sl st)

Make a slip knot with the new color (or yarn) and place loop on hook. Insert hook from front to back in the (usually) first stitch (unless specified otherwise). Yarn over and pull loop through stitch and loop on hook (slip stitch made).

Single Crochet (sc)

Starting with a loop on your hook, insert hook in stitch or space specified and draw up a loop (two loops on hook). Yarn over and pull yarn through both the loops on your hook (first sc made).

The height of a single crochet stitch is one chain high.

When working single crochet stitches into a foundation chain, begin the first single crochet in the second chain from the hook. The skipped chain stitch provides the height of the stitch.

At the beginning of a single crochet row or round, start by making one chain stitch (to get the height) and work the first single crochet stitch into first stitch

Note: The one chain stitch is never counted as a single crochet stitch.

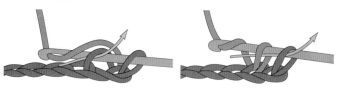

Half-Double Crochet (hdc)

Starting with a loop on your hook, yarn over hook before inserting hook in stitch or space specified and draw up a loop (three loops on hook). Yarn over and pull yarn through all three loops (first hdc made).

The height of a half-double crochet stitch is two chains high.

When working half-double crochet stitches into a foundation chain, begin the first stitch in the third chain from the hook. The two skipped chains provide the height. When starting a row or round with a half-double crochet stitch, make two chain stitches and work in the first stitch (Note: The two chain stitches are never counted as a half-double stitch).

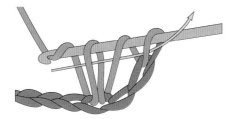

Double Crochet (dc)

Starting with a loop on your hook, yarn over hook before inserting hook in stitch or space specified and draw up a loop (three loops on hook). Yarn over and pull yarn through two loops (two loops remain on hook). Yarn over and pull yarn through remaining two loops on hook (first dc made).

The height of a double crochet stitch is three chains high.

When working double crochet stitches into a foundation chain, begin the first stitch in the fourth chain from the hook.

The three skipped chains count as the first double crochet stitch. When starting a row or round with a double crochet stitch, make three chain stitches (which count as the first double crochet), skip the first stitch (under the chains) and work a double crochet in the next (second) stitch. On the following row or round, when you work in the 'made' stitch, you will be working in the top chain (3rd chain stitch of the three chains).

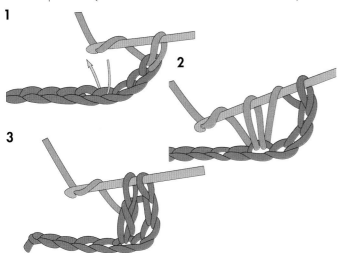

Treble (Or Triple) Crochet (tr)

Starting with a loop on your hook, yarn over hook twice before inserting hook in stitch or space specified and draw up a loop (four loops on hook). Yarn over and pull yarn through two loops (three loops remain on hook). Again, make a yarn over and pull yarn through two loops (two loops remain on hook). Once more, yarn over and pull through remaining two loops (first tr made).

The height of a treble crochet stitch is four chains high. When working treble crochet stitches into a foundation chain, begin the first stitch in the fifth chain from the hook. The four skipped chains count as the first treble crochet stitch. When starting a row or round with a treble crochet stitch, make four chain stitches (which count as the first treble crochet), skip the first stitch (under the chains) and work a treble crochet in the next (second) stitch. On the following row or round, when you work in the 'made' stitch, you will be working in the top chain (4th chain stitch of the four chains).

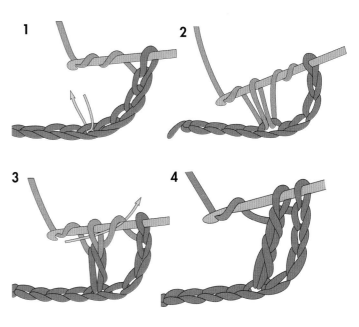

Special Stitches Used in Amigurumi

Invisible Single Crochet Decrease (sc-dec)

Insert the hook into the front loops of the next 2 stitches (3 loops on hook).

Yarn over and draw through first two loops on hook (2 loops remain on hook).

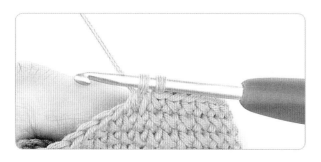

Yarn over and draw through both loops on hook (sc-dec made).

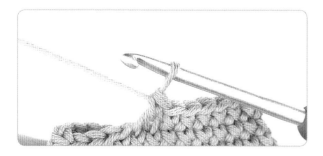

Note If you prefer, you can use the normal single crochet decrease stitch.

Single Crochet Decrease - "normal decrease" (sc2tog)

Insert hook in next stitch and pull up a loop, (two loops on hook).

Insert hook in next stitch and pull up a loop (three loops on hook).

Yarn over, draw through all three loops on hook.

Hint Use the invisible decrease (sc-dec) when working in the continuous spiral rounds and use the normal decrease (sc2tog) when working in rows.

Single Crochet Increase (inc)

Work 2 single crochet stitches in the same stitch indicated.

Single Crochet Double Increase (inc3)

Work 3 single crochet stitches in the same stitch indicated.

Crochet Techniques For Amigurumi

Back Ridge Of Foundation Chain

The back ridge (also called back bumps or back bars) is found on wrong side of the foundation chain. It consists of single loops behind the 'v-loops'. To work in the back ridge, one inserts the hook from front to back through the back ridge loop to pull up the yarn. Working in the Back Ridge gives a neater finish to projects.

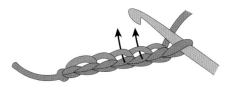

Changing Colors / Attaching New Yarn

With the current color, work the last stitch before the color change up to the last step of the stitch. Using the new color, yarn over hook, pull new color through remaining loops on hook.

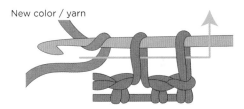

New color / yarn

Close The Opening

Working in the stitches of the last round, insert the yarn needle from back to front through the front loop of each stitch around. Gently pull the yarn to tighten the hole. Once the opening is closed, secure the yarn. Insert the needle back through the center of the ring and taking care (squashing the stuffing), bring it out at an inconspicuous place on the piece.

Work a few weaving stitches before inserting the needle back through the stuffed piece and out at another point. Cut the yarn close to the piece so that it retracts into the stuffing.

Fasten Off

After the last single crochet stitch is worked, work a slip stitch in the next stitch. Cut the yarn, leaving a tail. With the tail, yarn over and pull the tail through the stitch.

Fitting Safety Eyes / Nose

Choose and mark the positions for the eyes (or nose) on the front of the face. Insert the shank of the eye (or nose) through the fabric from right side to wrong side. (The eye is on the front side, the shank sticks out at the back.) Attach the locking washer onto the shank and push down firmly to lock it tightly. You can use a safety eye insertion tool for doing this.

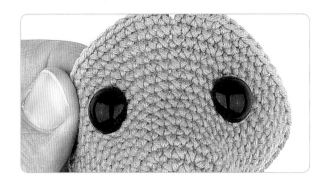

Front And Back Loops

Every stitch has what looks like 'v's on the top. There are two loops that make up the 'v'. The front loop is the loop closest to you and the back loop is the loop furthest from you. Generally, we work in both loops – under both the front and back loops. Working in either the front or back loops only, creates a decorative ridge (made up of the unworked loops).

Note Work all stitches under both loops unless otherwise instructed.

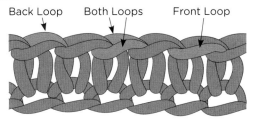

Back Loop   Both Loops   Front Loop

Invisible Join

After the last stitch is worked (do not slip stitch in next stitch), cut the yarn leaving a tail and pull the tail through the last stitch. Using the tail and a yarn needle, skip the next stitch and insert the needle under both loops of the following stitch. Then insert the needle into the back loop of the last stitch made (the same stitch where the tail came through) and also through the horizontal loop of the stitch (for stability). Gently tug the yarn so that it looks like a "stitch" and matches the others. Secure this "stitch" and weave in the tail.

Join With SC (Single Crochet Standing Stitch)

With a slip knot on hook, insert hook into stitch or space specified and pull up a loop (two loops on hook). Yarn over and pull through both loops on hook (first single crochet made).

Join with Slip Knot

Using the yarn, make a slip knot. Do not insert your hook through loop. Insert your hook in the stitch or space indicated and place the loop of the slip knot on the loop. Gently pull the loop through the stitch, keeping the knot at the back. Continue with the pattern.

Weaving in Yarn Tails

Thread the tail onto a yarn needle. Starting close to where the tail begins, preferably working on the wrong side, weave the tail through the back of stitches (preferably of the same color) to hide the yarn. When done, trim the tail close to the fabric.

For weaving in ends on an already stuffed pieces, you can secure the yarn close to the piece and then insert the needle through the stuffing and out the other side. If you want, you can do this a few times. When done, cut the yarn close to the toy and let the end disappear inside.

Magic Ring (Or Adjustable Ring)

1 Form a loop with the yarn, keeping the tail end of the yarn behind the working yarn (the yarn attached to the ball).

2 Insert the hook through the loop (from front to back), and pull the working yarn through the loop (from back to front). Do not tighten up the loop.

3 Using the working yarn, make a chain stitch (to secure the ring). This chain stitch does NOT count as first stitch.

4 Work the required stitches into the ring (over the tail strand). When all the stitches are done, gently tug the tail end to close the ring, before joining the round (if specified). Remember, make sure this tail is firmly secured before weaving in the end.

Note If you prefer, you can use any type of "ring" to start your project (or start with ch-2, and working the first round in the second chain from hook). The advantage of using the adjustable Magic Ring, is that when it is tightened, it closes the hole completely.

Tip Secure your Magic Ring after the first few rounds and before you start stuffing.

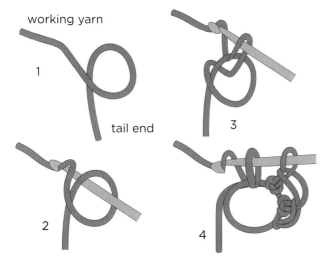

working yarn

1

tail end

2

3

4

Jointed Toys

Instead of plastic doll joints, you can use cotter pin joints, buttons and thread, or even just thread.

Using Plastic Doll Joints

Each joint consists of three pieces – a disc with a stem, a washer, and a fastener.

The disc with a stem in inserted from inside the limbs, with the stem protruding through the fabric.

The stem is then inserted into the Body. First place the washer over the stem, and then the fastener.

Making Button and Thread Joints

The thread used should be very strong and able to withstand a lot of tension. Cotton embroidery floss, nylon sewing thread (doubled or tripled) or even fishing line, works really well.

Cut a length of strong thread/yarn and draw through holes in button

Place the button inside the limb and using yarn needle, draw the doubled thread through the fabric.

Insert the yarn needle with doubled thread into the Body. Place another button inside the body and draw each thread through a different hole in the button. Knot the thread tails together.

Embriodery Stitches

When embroidering on crochet, it is recommended to insert the needle through the yarn of the stitch and not through the 'holes' between the stitches. This makes it easier to control the placement of the embroidery thread.

Back Stitch

Bring threaded needle up from wrong to right side of fabric (#1). Insert needle back down a bit before (#2) and bring it out a bit ahead (#3) on the desired outline. Insert the needle back down through the same hole (#1) and bring it out a bit ahead again. Repeat along the desired outline.

Bullion Stitch

Bring threaded needle up from wrong to right side of fabric at the position where you want the knot to start (#1). Insert the needle back into the fabric at the position where you want the knot to end (#2) and back up through the starting point (#1) – without pulling the needle through. Wrap the yarn/thread around tip of needle as many times as needed. Hold the wrapped loops as you gently pull the needle through the fabric and loops to form the Knot. Insert the needle back through the fabric to the wrong side.

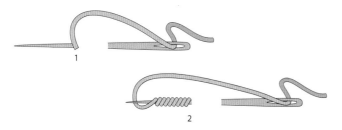

Note To form a Bullion Knot with a slight curve, make more wraps around the tip of the needle than are needed.

French Knot

Bring threaded needle up from wrong to right side of fabric at the position where you want the knot (#1). Wrap the yarn/thread twice around needle. Insert the needle back through the fabric, close to where it came up (almost in the same hole as #1). Gently pull the needle and yarn/thread through the wrapped loops to form the knot.

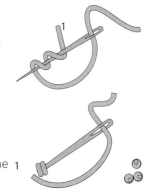

Satin Stitch

Bring threaded needle up from wrong to right side of fabric (#1). Insert needle along desired outline (#2) and bring it out close to #1. Insert it back, close to #2 and out close to previous stitch. Repeat making stitches close to each other following the desired shape. Take care to make even stitches that are not too tight, so that the fabric still lies flat.

Straight Stitch

Bring threaded needle up from wrong to right side of fabric at the position you want to start the stitch. Insert the needle back into the fabric at the position you want to end the stitch. Repeat for the remaining stitches.

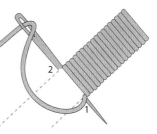

Assembling Amigurumi Pieces Together

Sewing all the amigurumi pieces together can sometimes be a daunting task.
Have no fear! There are lots of resources available on the internet showing you how it can be done.

Identifying the Pieces

There are generally three types of pieces that need joining:

1 An "open" piece - where the last round has not been closed. This can be a Body, a Head or even a Limb.

2 A "flat" piece – this is where either where the last round is folded together and crocheted or sewn closed, or it is a single thickness fabric.

3 The other type is what is known as a "closed" piece. This is usually a finished, stuffed piece. Generally, you would attach another piece to this one. Think of a finished, stuffed Body where you need to attach the limbs. You sew through the stitches of the fabric of a closed piece, not through the tops of stitches.

Types of Joining Needed

"Open" to "Open"

This could be where you are joining the last round at the top of the Body to the last round of the neck on the Head. Usually the pieces end up with the same stitch count in the last row and when you join them together you match them, stitch for stitch. One way of sewing this join is using the whipstitch.

"Open" to "Closed"

Examples of this would be joining "open", stuffed limbs to the "closed" Body, or sewing a Muzzle (open) to the face on a Head (closed).

"Flat" to "Closed"

With a Body or Head as the "closed' piece, the Ears, long limbs and Tails could be the "flat" pieces needing attaching.

Ways of Sewing Joins

There are many different sewing stitches you can use to join pieces together. Everyone develops their own preferences. Practice the various sewing stitch techniques and see which ones you like and which one(s) gives you the nicest finish.

As mentioned, the internet is a great help to identify the "right" sewing stitch for the job and has many tutorials for them. However, the basic stitches used are the Whipstitch and Mattress Stitch (or variation thereof).

General Tips When Stitching Pieces Together

1 Make sure both pieces you are sewing together are either right-side facing or wrong-side facing (whichever the pattern call for), unless otherwise instructed.

2 When attaching the Head or Limbs to the Body, make sure they are facing the correct way (unless the pattern says differently). For example, the feet on the Legs should usually point to the front of the body.

3 Use straight pins, stuck straight down into a stuffed piece, to position pieces before sewing.

Hint Try placing and pinning the pieces in different positions to give your toy a different 'look'. Once you're happy with the position, you can then sew the pieces together.

4 Where possible, use the same color yarn of at least one of the pieces getting sewn together.

5 When you need to use a separate strand of yarn for sewing the pieces together (not a yarn tail from either piece), start by leaving a long tail for sewing in later. You can tug this tail gently as you go to keep your stitches neat. When you've finished sewing the joins, go back and secure and weave in the front tail.

Hint By doing it this way, it is easier to pull out and fix things if you make a mistake, than trying to unpick a secured starting point.

Whipstitch

This stitch is commonly used to join "open" to "open" pieces.

With both pieces right-side facing, insert your needle through a crocheted stitch on the first piece, from front to back.

Step 1 Bring the needle up through the corresponding stitch on the second piece, from back to front.

Step 2 Insert your needle in the next stitch on the first piece from front to back. Repeat Steps 1 & 2.

Mattress Stitch

This is a very versatile stitch and can be virtually "invisible" when tugged gently. It can be used for joining most of the types of pieces together.

Both pieces should be right-side facing. Starting on the first piece, insert your needle under a crocheted stitch, from front to back to front. On the corresponding stitch on the second piece, insert the needle from front to back to front under the stitch.

Step 1 On the first piece, insert your needle in the same place where it came out and bring it up under the next stitch.

Step 2 On the second piece, insert your needle in the same place where it came out and bring it up under the next stitch.

Repeat steps 1 & 2.

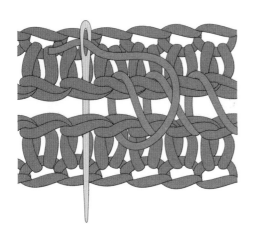

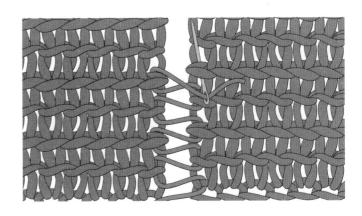

Projects

stacy

Sporty and Sweet

designer

Dilek Birkan
@dlkbrkn

Materials & Tools

HELLO Cotton Yarn

For Doll

» **Main Color (MC):** Dark Beige (158) - for Body
» **Color A:** White (154) - Socks & Underwear
» **Color B:** Brown (126) - for Hair
» **Color C:** Salmon (109) - for Cheeks

Shorts, Blouse, Peak Cap & Shoes

» **Color D:** Gray Blue (149)
» **Color E:** Sea Green (136)

Dress, Ribbon & Shoes

» **Color B:** Brown (126) - for Head Band
» **Color F:** Nectarine (115)
» **Color G:** (101) Baby Pink
» **Color H:** (160) Black

Hook Size

» 2.5 mm hook

Other

» Stitch Markers
» Yarn Needle
» Stuffing
» Straight Pins
» DMC Embroidery Floss - Black (for Eyes)
» Embroidery Needle

Finished Size
About 10½" (27 cm) tall

Skill Level
Intermediate

SPECIAL STITCHES & TECHNIQUES

Single Crochet Decrease over 3 Stitches: (sc3tog):

[Insert hook in next stitch and pull up a loop] 3 times **(4 loops on hook),** yarn over and draw through all four loops. Decrease made.

Bobble (bob): Yarn over, insert hook in stitch or space specified and draw up a loop **(3 loops on hook),** yarn over and draw through two loops on hook **(2 loops remain),** yarn over and insert hook in same stitch or space and draw up a loop **(4 loops on hook),** yarn over and draw through two loops on hook **(3 loops remain),** yarn over and draw through all three loops. Bobble made.

Button: [Ch 3, **bob** in 3rd ch from hook] twice, sl st in same ch as first bobble made.

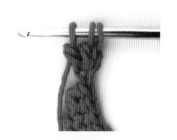   

DOLL

Note: In the photos, pink yarn is used in place of a stitch marker.

BODY

Sock (Make 2)

Note: The first round is important to form the sock neatly!

Round 1: With **Color A,** ch 8, starting in 2nd ch from hook, sc in each of next 6 ch, 3 sc in last ch; working on other side of starting chain, sc in each of next 6 ch. (15 sc)
Do not join. Mark last st made. Move marker at the end of each round.

Round 2: Inc in next st, sc in each of next 5 sts, inc in each of next 3 sts, sc in each of next 5 sts, inc in next st. (20 sc)

Round 3: Inc in next st, sc in each of next 7 sts, inc in each of next 4 sts, sc in each of next 7 sts, inc in next st. (26 sc)

Round 4: Working in **back loops** only, sc in each st around. (26 sc) *(image 1)*

Round 5: Sc in each of next 7 sts, [dec] 6 times, sc in each of next 7 sc. (20 sc)

Round 6: Sc in each of next 7 sts, [dec] 3 times, sc in each of next 7 sc. (17 sc)

Round 7: Sc in each of next 5 sts, **sc3tog**, sc in next st, **sc3tog**, sc in each of next 5 sts. (13 sc)

Round 8: Sc in each of next 6 sts, dec, sc in each of next 5 sts. (12 sc)

Rounds 9-10: (2 rounds) Sc in each st around. (12 sc)
At the end of Round 10, move the marker to the back loop only of the last st.

Round 11: Working in **front loops** only, [ch 2, sc in next st] 12 times. *(image 2)* (12 sc & 12 ch-2 lps) Do not move marker. Fasten off and weave in all ends. *(image 3)*

- Stuff Sock firmly

Leg (Make 2)

Join **MC** to marked back loop on Round 10 of Sock. Move marker at the end of each round. *(image 4)*

Rounds 1-2: (2 rounds) Sc in each st around. (12 sc)

Round 3: Sc in each of next 2 sts, inc in next st, sc in each of next 9 sts. (13 sc)

Rounds 4-11: (8 rounds) Sc in each st around. (13 sc)

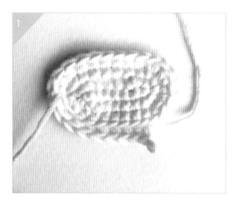  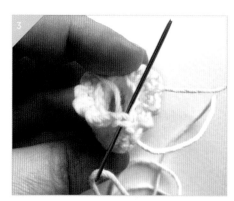

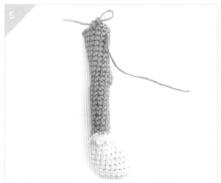
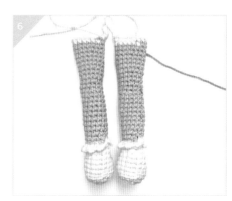

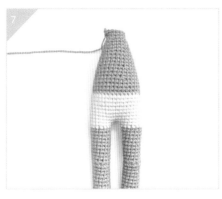

Round 12: Sc in each of next 3 sts, dec, sc in each of next 4 sts, inc in each of next 3 sts **(knee)**, sc in next st. (15 sc)

Round 13: Sc in each of next 8 sts, [dec] 3 times, sc in next st. (12 sc)

Round 14: Sc in each of next 4 sts, inc in next st, sc in each of next 7 sts. (13 sc)

Rounds 15-16: (2 rounds) Sc in each st around. (13 sc)

Round 17: Sc in each of next 5 sts, inc in next st, sc in each of next 7 sts. (14 sc)

Rounds 18-20: (3 rounds) Sc in each st around. (14 sc)

Round 21: Sc in each of next 6 sts, inc in next st, sc in each of next 7sts. (15 sc)

Round 22: Sc in each st around. (15 sc) *(image 5)*

Round 23: Sc in each of next 5 sts, change to **Color A,** sc in each of net 10 sts. (15 sc) Fasten off MC.

For First Leg Only:

Round 24: Sc in each of next 5 sts. Move marker to last st made. Fasten off Color A.

For Second Leg:

Round 24: Sc in each of next 13 sts. Do not fasten off.

- Stuff both Legs firmly. *(image 6)*

Body

Round 25: *(Joining Legs)* Ch 2, working on First Leg, sc in marked st, sc in each of next 14 sts, working in ch-2, sc in each of next 2 ch, working on Second Leg, sc in each of next 15 sts, working on other side of ch-2, sc in each of next 2 ch. (34 sc) Mark last st made. Move marker

at the end of each round.

Rounds 26-33: *(8 rounds)* Sc in each st around. (34 sc)

Round 34: Change to **MC**, sc in each st around. (34 sc)

Round 35: Sc in each of next 7 sts, dec, sc in each of next 15 sts, dec, sc in each of next 8 sts. (32 sc)

Rounds 36-37: *(2 rounds)* Sc in each st around. (32 sc)

Round 38: [Sc in each of next 6 sts, dec] 4 times. (28 sc)

Rounds 39-40: *(2 rounds)* Sc in each st around. (28 sc)

Round 41: [Sc in each of next 5 sts, dec] 4 times. (24 sc)

Rounds 42-43: *(2 rounds)* Sc in each st around. (24 sc)

Round 44: [Sc in each of next 4 sts, dec] 4 times. (20 sc)

Rounds 45-46: *(2 rounds)* Sc in each st around. (20 sc)

Round 47: [Sc in each of next 3 sts, dec] 4 times. (16 sc)

Round 48: Sc in each st around. (16 sc)

- Stuff Body firmly.

Round 49: [Sc in each of next 2 sts, dec] 4 times. (12 sc)

Round 50: Sc in each st around. (12 sc) Do not fasten off. *(image 7)*

HEAD

Continuing from Body, moving marker at the end of each round.

Round 1: [Inc in next st] 12 times. (24 sc)

Round 2: [Sc in next st, inc in next st] 12 times. (36 sc)

Round 3: [Sc in each of next 5 sts, inc in next st] 6 times. (42 sc)

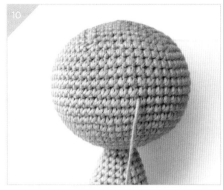

Round 4: [Sc in each of next 6 sts, inc in next st] 6 times. (48 sc)

Round 5: Sc in each of next 3 sts, inc in next st, [sc in each of next 7 sts, inc in next st] 5 times, sc in each of next 4 sts. (54 sc)

Round 6: [Sc in each of next 8 sts, inc in next st] 6 times. (60 sc)

Rounds 7-15: *(9 rounds)* Sc in each st around. (60 sc) *(image 8)*

Round 16: [Sc in each of next 8 sts, dec] 6 times. (54 sc)

Round 17: [Sc in each of next 7 sts, dec] 6 times. (48 sc)

Round 18: [Sc in each of next 6 sts, dec] 6 times. (42 sc)

Round 19: [Sc in each of next 5 sts, dec] 6 times. (36 sc)

Round 20: [Sc in each of next 4 sts, dec] 6 times. (30 sc)

Round 21: [Sc in each of next 3 sts, dec] 6 times. (24 sc)

Round 22: [Sc in each of next 2 sts, dec] 6 times. (18 sc)

Stuff Head firmly.

Round 23: [Sc in next st, dec] 6 times. (12 sc)

Round 24: [Dec] 6 times. (6 sc) Fasten off, leaving a long tail to close the opening (and embroider the Nose later).

Using the tail and a yarn needle, close the opening securely. *(image 9)* Insert the needle back through the center of the Head, bringing it out at the Nose position. Remove the needle and leave the yarn hanging for now. *(image 10)*

ARM (Make 2)

Round 1: With **MC**, make a magic ring, 6 sc in ring. (6 sc) Do not join. Mark last st. Move marker at the end of each round.

Round 2: [Sc in each of next 2 sts, inc in next st] 2 times. (8 sc)

Round 3: [Sc in each of next 3 sts, inc in next st] 2 times. (10 sc)

Rounds 4-5: *(2 rounds)* Sc in each st around. (10 sc)

Round 6: [Sc in each of next 3 sts, dec] 2 times. (8 sc)

Rounds 7-25: *(19 rounds)* Sc in each st around. (8 sc)

Last Row: Flatten the Arm. Working through both thicknesses, sc in each of next 3 sts. Fasten off, leaving a long tail for sewing.

Position and pin the Arms to either side of the Body, and sew in place. *(image 11-14)*

HAIR

Note: *The magic ring is only closed once all the Hair and Bangs are complete.*

With **Color B,** leaving a long tail for sewing, make a large magic ring.

Row 1: Ch 32, hdc in 3rd st from hook, hdc in each of next 5 ch, sc in each of next 24 ch, sc in magic ring. *(image 15-17)*

Row 2: Ch 1, turn, working in **back loops** only, sc in each of next 24 sts. Leave remaining sts unworked. *(image 18)*

Row 3: Ch 8, hdc in 3rd ch from hook, hdc in each of next 5 ch, working in **back loops** only, sc in each of next 24 sts, sc in magic ring. *(image 19-21)*

Rows 4-39: Repeat Rows 2-3 eighteen times.

At the end of Row 39, there are 19 long hair strands.

Bangs

Row 40: Ch 1, turn, working in **back loops** only, sc in each of next 11 sts. Leave remaining sts unworked.

Row 41: Ch 2, turn, working in **back loops** only, sc in each of next 11 sts, sc in magic ring.

Rows 42-53: Repeat Rows 40-41 six times. At the end of Row 53, fasten off, leaving a long tail for sewing. (*image 22*)

Close the magic ring tightly, and secure it. Using the tail and yarn needle, sew the last row of Bangs to the first 11 chain stitches at beginning of Hair.

Position and pin the Hair on the Head, and sew in place.

CHEEKS (Make 2)

Round 1: With **Color C**, make a magic ring; 8 sc in ring; join with sl st to first sc. (8 sc) Fasten off, leaving a long tail for sewing. (*image 26*)

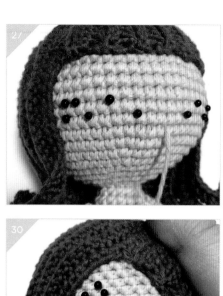

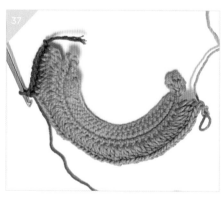

FINISHING THE FACE

Pin out the position of each Eye and the Eyelashes. *(image 27)*

Using the hanging yarn tail, embroider the Nose with a few small, straight stitches. *(image 28)*

Using the Black Floss, embroider the Eyes and Eyelashes. *(image 29-32)*

Pin the Cheeks in position, and using long tail, sew in place. *(image 33)*

SPORTY OUTFIT

SHORTS

Legs (Make 2)

Round 1: With **Color D**, ch 23, join with sl st to first ch to form a ring; sc in each ch around. (23 sc) Do not join. Mark last st. Move marker at the end of each round.

Rounds 2-3: *(2 rounds)* Sc in each st around. (23 sc)

At the end of Round 3, for first Leg, fasten off. Do not fasten off for second Leg.

Shorts

Round 4: *(Joining Legs)* Sc in each st around, working in first Leg, sc in each st around. (46 sc) *(image 34)* Mark last st. Move marker at the end of each round.

Rounds 5-10: *(6 rounds)* Sc in each st around. (46 sc) *(image 35)*

Round 11: Sc in each of next 5 sts, dec, [sc in each of next 9 sts, dec] 3 times, sc in each of next 6 sts. (42 sc)

Rounds 12-15: *(4 rounds)* Sc in each st around. (42 sc)

At the end of Round 15, fasten off and weave in ends.

BLOUSE

Row 1: With *Color E*, ch 31, starting in 2nd ch from hook, sc in each ch across. (30 sc)

Row 2: *(Right Side)* Ch 7, turn, sc in each st across, make **button**. (30 sc, ch-7 lp & button)

Row 3: Ch 1, turn, sc in each st across. (30 sc)

Row 4: Ch 2, turn, 2 dc in each st across; *(image 36)* join with sl st in first dc. (60 dc) Remove hook. Do not fasten off.

Row 5: Do not turn. Join **Color D** in first st on Row 4, sc in each st across. *(image 37)* (60 sc) Remove hook.

Work continues in rounds.

Round 6: Do not turn. Pick up **Color E**, ch 2, working in **back loops** only, starting in 1st st on Row 5, *(image 38)* [dc in next st, 2 dc, in next st] around; join with sl st to first dc. (90 dc)

Round 7: Pick up **Color D**, ch 1, sc in each st around; join with sl st to first sc. (90 sc)

Round 8: Pick up **Color E**, ch 2, working in **back loops** only, dc in each st around; join with sl st to first dc. Fasten off and weave in all ends.

Neck Tie

With **Color D**, ch 40, with right side of Blouse facing, working across neckline, starting in 13th ch, sc in each of next 5 ch, ch 40. Fasten off and weave in all ends. *(image 39)*

PEAK CAP

Round 1: With **Color D**, ch 61, join with sl st to first ch to form a ring; ch 2, dc in each ch around; join with sl st to first dc. (61 dc) Remove hook. Do not fasten off. *(image 40)*

Row 1: Join **Color E** with sc to front loop only of 20th st, working in **front loops** only, sc in each of next 21 sts. (22 sc) *(image 41)*

Row 2: Ch 1, turn, Sc in each of next 3 sts, hdc in each of next 16 sts, sc in each of next 3 sts. (22 sts)

Row 3: Ch 1, turn, dec *(using first 2 sts)*, sc in each of next 3 sts, hdc in each of next 12 sts, sc in each of next 3 sts, dec *(using last 2 sts)*. (20 sts)

Row 4: Ch 1, turn, dec *(using first 2 sts)*, sc in each of next 3 sts, hdc in each of next 10 sts, sc in each of next 3 sts, dec *(using last 2 sts)*. (18 sts)

Row 5: Ch 1, turn, dec *(using first 2 sts)*, sc in each of next 14 sts, dec *(using last 2 sts)*. (16 sts) Fasten off Color E.

Round 2: Pick up **Color D**, ch 1, sc in each stitch and row around; join. Fasten off and weave in all ends.

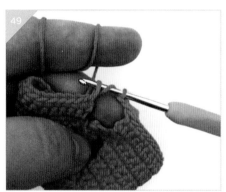

SHOES (Make 2)

Round 1: With **Color E,** ch 8, starting in 2nd ch from hook, sc in each of next 6 ch, 3 sc in last ch; working on other side of starting chain, sc in each of next 6 ch. (15 sc) Do not join. Mark last st made. Move marker at the end of each round.

Round 2: Inc in next st, sc in each of next 5 sts, inc in each of next 3 sts, sc in each of next 5 sts, inc in next st. (20 sc)

Round 3: Inc in next st, sc in each of next 6 sts, inc in each of next 6 sts, sc in each of next 6 sts, inc in next st. (28 sc)

Round 4: Working in **back loops** only, sc in each st around. (28 sc) *(image 44)*

Rounds 5-7: *(3 rounds)* Sc in each st around. (28 sc)

Round 8: Sc in each of next 7 sts, [dec] 7 times, sc in each of next 7 sts. (21 sc)

Round 9: Change to **Color D**, sc in each st around. (21 sc) Fasten off and weave in all ends. *(image 45)*

Sole Edging

Working in unused front loops on Round 3, join **Color D** with sc to any st, [sc in next st] around. (28 sc) Fasten off with Needle Join and weave in ends.

Shoe Button

With **Color D**, make a magic ring; 6 sc in ring; join with sl st to first sc. Fasten off, leaving a long tail for sewing.

Position and sew a button on each shoe. *(image 46)*

SWEET OUTFIT

DRESS

Row 1: *(Right Side)* With **Color F**, ch 35, starting in 2nd ch from hook, sc in each of next 34 ch. (34 sc)

Row 2: Ch 7, turn, sc in each of next 4 sts, ch 6, skip next 8 sts, sc in each of next 10 sts, ch 6, skip next 8 sts, sc in each of next 4 sts, make **button**. *(image 47-48)* (18 sc, 2 ch-6 lps, ch-7 lp & button)

Row 3: Turn, sc in each of next 4 sts, sc in **back loops** only of next 6 ch, sc in each of next 10 sts, sc in **back loops** only of next 6 ch, sc in each of next 4 sts. (30 sc)

Rows 4-6: *(3 rows)* Ch 1, turn, sc in each st across. (30 sc)

Row 7: Ch 1, turn, inc in first st, sc in each of next 5 sts, inc in next st, sc in each of next 16 sts, inc in next st, sc in each of next 5 sts, inc in last st. (34 sc)

Row 8: Ch 7, turn, sc in each of next 7 sts, inc in next st, sc in each of next 18 sts, inc in next st, sc in each of next 7 sts, **button**. (36 sc, ch-7 lp & button)

Row 9: Turn, inc in first st, sc in each of next 7 sts, inc in next st, sc in each of next 18 sts, inc in next st, sc in each of next 7 sts, inc in last st. (40 sc)

Rows 10-11: *(2 rows)* Ch 1, turn, sc in each st across. (40 sc) Work continues in Rounds.

Round 12: Ch 2, do not turn, 2 dc in first st on Row 11, dc in next st, [2 dc in next st, dc in next st] around; join with sl st to first dc. (60 dc) *(image 49-50)*

Round 13: Ch 2, 2 dc in same st as joining, [2 dc in next st] around; join with sl st to first dc. (120 dc)

Rounds 14-16: *(3 rounds)* Ch 2, dc in each st around; join with sl st to first dc. (120 dc)

Round 17: Ch 1, sc in same st as joining, [ch 3, skip next st, sc in next st] around, ending with ch 3, join with sl st to first sc. (60 sc & 60 ch-3 lps) Fasten off Color F and weave in ends.

Round 18: Working behind ch-3 lps on Round 17, join **Color G** with sc to first skipped st, [ch 3, sc in next skipped st] around, ending with ch 3; join with sl st to first sc. (60 sc & 60 ch-3 lps) Fasten off Color G and weave in ends. *(image 51-52)*

HAIR RIBBON

Head Band

With **Color B**, ch 61, join with sl st to first ch to form ring, sc in each of next 4 ch. Fasten off and weave in all ends

Ribbon

Row 1: With **Color F**, ch 15, starting in 2nd ch from hook, sc in each of next 14 ch. (14 sc)

Rows 2-11: *(10 rows)* Ch 1, turn, sc in each st across. (14 sc)

At the end of Row 11, do not fasten off. *(image 53)*

Edging

Round 1: Ch 1, turn, sc in first st, [ch 3, skip next st or row, sc in next st or row] around, ending with ch 3; join with sl st to first sc. Fasten off Color F and weave in ends.

Round 2: Working behind ch-3 lps on Round 1, join **Color G** with sc to first skipped st, [ch 3, sc in next st or row] around, ending with ch 3; join with sl st to first sc. Fasten off Color G and weave in ends. *(image 54)*

Ribbon Band

Row 1: With **Color G**, ch 15, starting in 4th ch from hook, dc in each ch across. Fasten off, leaving a long tail for sewing. *(image 55)*

Wrap the Ribbon Band around the Ribbon and Head Band together. Using the long tail and yarn needle, sew in place. *(image 56)*

BLACK SHOES (Make 2)

Round 1: With **Color H**, ch 8, starting in 2nd ch from hook, sc in each of next 6 ch, 3 sc in last ch; working on other side of starting chain, sc in each of next 6 ch. (15 sc) Do not join. Mark last st made. Move marker at the end of each round.

Round 2: Inc in next st, sc in each of next 5 sts, inc in each of next 3 sts, sc in each of next 5 sts, inc in next st. (20 sc)

Round 3: Inc in next st, sc in each of next 6 sts, inc in each of next 6 sts, sc in each of next 6 sts, inc in next st. (28 sc)

Round 4: Working in *back loops* only, sc in each st around. (28 sc)

Rounds 5-6: *(2 rounds)* Sc in each st around. (28 sc)

Round 7: Sc in each of next 7 sts, [dec] 7 times, sc in each of next 7 sts. (21 sc)

Round 8: Sc in each of next 7 sts, ch 6, skip next 7 sts, sc in each of next 7 sts. (14 sc & ch-6 lp) Fasten off and weave in all ends. *(image 57)*

flynn and abby
The Baby Doll Twins

designer
Mei Li Lee
@amigurumei

Materials & Tools

HELLO Cotton Yarn

For Each Dolls

» **Main Color (MC):** Cream (156) - for Head & Cheek Pouches

» **Color A:** Off-White (155) - for Hands, Feet & Collar

» **Color B:** Baby Pink (101) - for Cheeks

» **Color C:** Dusty Blue (145) - for Paw Pads

For Girl Doll

» **Color E:** Pink (103) - for Outfit

» **Color F:** Cherry Red (113) - for Cherries

» **Color G:** (133) Green - for Cherry Stems

For Boy Doll

» **Color D:** Dusty Blue (145) - for Bow Tie

» **Color H:** Yellow (123) - for Outfit

Hook Size

» 2.5 mm hook

Other

For Each Dolls

» Stitch Markers

» Yarn Needle

» Stuffing

» Straight Pins

» Safety Eyes - Black Oval (8mm by 6mm) x 2

» Safety Eye - Small Black Round (3mm) x 1 - for Nose

» DMC Embroidery Floss – Black

» Embroidery Needle

» Small piece of White Felt – to cut out for Eyes

» Craft Glue

For Boy Doll

» Turquoise Round Brads (4mm) x 3 – for Buttons

Optional

» Weighted Stuffing Beads (Poly-Pellets)

» Nylon Ankle-High Stockings (to hold Stuffing Beads)

Finished Size
About 10½" (27 cm) tall

Skill Level
Intermediate

Special Stitches & Techniques

Invisible Decrease (inv-dec): Insert hook under the front loop of each of the next 2 stitches. Yarn over and pull the yarn through these 2 front loops (2 loops remain on hook). Yarn over and draw through both loops on hook.

French Knot: Bring threaded needle up from the wrong to right side of piece at the position where you want the knot (#1). Wrap the yarn around the needle the required number of times and insert the needle back through the piece close to where it came out (almost is the same hole as #1). Gently pull the needle and yarn through the wrapped loops to form the knot.

Pattern Notes:

1. All parts are worked in spiral rounds, except for the Collar, the Boy's Hair, and the Bowtie.

2. The patterns for the Head, Hood, Body, Collar, Arms, and Legs are the same for both dolls.

DOLL

HEAD

Round 1: With **MC**, make a magic ring, 6 sc in ring. (6 sc)

Round 2: Inc in each st around. (12 sc)

Round 3: [Inc in next st, sc in next st] 6 times. (18 sc)

Round 4: [Inc in next st, sc in each of next 2 sts] 6 times. (24 sc)

Round 5: [Inc in next st, sc in each of next 3 sts] 6 times. (30 sc)

Round 6: [Inc in next st, sc in each of next 4 sts] 6 times. (36 sc)

Round 7: [Inc in next st, sc in each of next 5 sts] 6 times. (42 sc)

Round 8: [Inc in next st, sc in each of next 6 sts] 6 times. (48 sc)

Round 9: [Inc in next st, sc in each of next 7 sts] 6 times. (54 sc)

Round 10: [Inc in next st, sc in each of next 8 sts] 6 times. (60 sc)

Round 11: [Inc in next st, sc in each of next 9 sts] 6 times. (66 sc)

Round 12: [Inc in next st, sc in each of next 10 sts] 6 times. (72 sc)

Rounds 13-23: *(11 rounds)* Sc in each st around. (72 sc)

Round 24: [Inv-dec, sc in each of next 10 sts] 6 times. (66 sc)

Round 25: [Inv-dec, sc in each of next 9 sts] 6 times. (60 sc)

Note: For a safer alternative, insert and secure the Safety Eyes at this point between Rounds 19 & 20, with 11 stitches between them. Remember to pair them with a piece of white felt before securing them completely. Do not forget to attach half moon shape cut felts under the eyes fitting with the size of eyes.

Insert and secure the Safety Nose between Rounds 20 & 21, centered between the Eyes.

Round 26: [Inv-dec, sc in each of next 8 sts] 6 times. (54 sc)

Round 27: [Inv-dec, sc in each of next 7 sts] 6 times. (48 sc)

Round 28: [Inv-dec, sc in each of next 6 sts] 6 times. (42 sc)

Round 29: [Inv-dec, sc in each of next 5 sts] 6 times. (36 sc)

Round 30: [Inv-dec, sc in each of next 4 sts] 6 times. (30 sc)

Round 31: [Inv-dec, sc in each of next 3 sts] 6 times. (24 sc)

Round 32: [Inv-dec, sc in each of next 2 sts] 6 times. (18 sc)

Start stuffing Head, adding more as you go.

Round 33: [Inv-dec, sc in next st] 6 times. (12 sc)

Round 34: [Inv-dec] 6 times. (6 sc) Fasten off leaving a long tail to close the opening (and to make Eye indentations).

Using the tail and a yarn needle, close the opening securely. Remove the needle and leave the yarn hanging for now.

CHEEK POUCH (Make 2)

Round 1: With **MC**, make a magic ring, 6 sc in ring. (6 sc)

Round 2: Inc in each st around. (12 sc)

Round 3: [Inc in next st, sc in next st] 6 times. (18 sc)

Round 4: Sc in each st around. (18 sc) Fasten off with a Needle Join, leaving a long tail for sewing.

CHEEK (Make 2)

Round 1: With **Color C**, make a magic ring, 6 sc in ring. (6 sc) Tug tail to tighten ring. Do not join.

Round 2: Inc in each st around. (12 sc) Fasten off with a Needle Join, leaving a long tail for sewing.

FINISHING THE FACE

Eye Indentations

Note: *This may be omitted if the Safety Eyes have already been inserted.*

1. Using Straight Pins, mark the position of the eyes between Rounds 19 & 20, with 11 stitches between them. Using a yarn needle and the yarn tail on Head, insert the

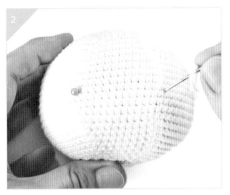
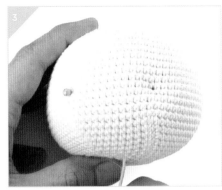
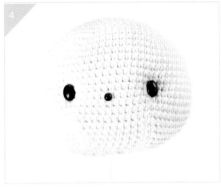
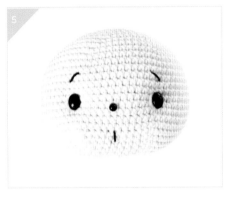

needle from the bottom, bringing it out next to the marked Eye position on the left side of the face. *(image 1-2)*

2. Insert the needle back into the Head in the next stitch, bringing it out at the bottom of the Head. Gently tug on the yarn to create a slight indentation. *(image 3)*

3. Repeat for the right side of the Head. Secure the yarn tail with a knot at the base of the Head and trim the excess yarn. You may use your thumbs to gently add pressure to deepen the indentations.

Eyes, Nose, Eyebrows & Mouth

1. Cut out two small half-moons of the White Felt to match the size of your oval Eyes.

2. Insert the shaft of the Eye into the Eye indentation, positioning the one half-moon of White Felt, before pushing the Eye all the way in. Add glue to secure Eye in place. Repeat for other Eye.

Note: *Both the Eye Whites should be on same side of each Eye, either the left side or the right side, depending on which direction you want the doll to look at.*

3. Add glue to the shaft of the Nose and insert it in the center of the face below Round 20, between the Eyes (with five stitches between Eye and Nose on each side). *(image 4)*

4. Using the Floss, embroider the Eyebrows (above each Eye) with a diagonal straight stitch, from the top to the bottom of Round 16 and 2 stitches wide. Then make the mouth.

5. You may choose either a "smile" or a "surprised" look for the mouth. To make the "smile", embroider a loose horizontal backstitch, 5 stitches wide, centered under the

Nose below Round 23. Dab on some glue to shape and secure the "smile". For a "surprised" look, embroider a vertical straight stitch over 2 rounds under the Nose. *(image 5-6)*

Cheek Pouches & Cheeks

1. Position the Cheek Pouches to the sides of each Eye between Rounds 21 & 25, and sew in place, then bring the yarn out at base of Head. Knot to secure and trim the ends.

2. Position the Cheeks below each Eye and sew in place, then bring the yarn out at base of Head. Knot to secure and trim the ends. *(image 7)*

HAIR - for Girl

First Piece

Round 1: With **Color B**, make a magic ring, 6 sc in ring. (6 sc)

Round 2: Inc in each st around. (12 sc)

Round 3: [Inc in next st, sc in next st] 6 times. (18 sc)

Round 4: [Inc in next st, sc in each of next 2 sts] 6 times. (24 sc)

Round 5: [Inc in next st, sc in each of next 3 sts] 6 times. (30 sc)

Round 6: [Inc in next st, sc in each of next 4 sts] 6 times. (36 sc)

Round 7: [Inc in next st, sc in each of next 5 sts] 6 times. (42 sc) Fasten off, leaving a long tail for sewing.

Second Piece

Rounds 1-7: Repeat Rounds 1-7 of First Piece.
At the end of Round 7, do not fasten off.

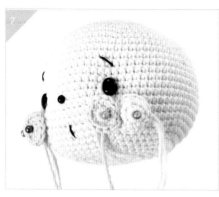

Round 8: [Inc in next st, sc in each of next 6 sts] 6 times. (48 sc)

Round 9: [Inc in next st, sc in each of next 7 sts] 6 times. (54 sc)

Round 10: [Inc in next st, sc in each of next 8 sts] 6 times. (60 sc)

Round 11: [Inc in next st, sc in each of next 9 sts] 6 times. (66 sc) Fasten off, leaving a long tail for sewing.

HAIR – for Boy

Row 1: With **Color B**, ch 12, starting in 2nd ch from hook, sc in each ch across. (11 sc)

Rows 2-17: *(16 rows)* Ch 1, turn, sc in each st across. (11 sc) At the end of Row 17, fasten off, leaving a long tail for sewing.

ATTACHING HAIR

1. For Girl: Place both pieces on top of Head, having the second piece overlapping the smaller first piece, and positioning the "bangs" slightly above the eyebrows.
(image 8)

2. Using tails and yarn needle, secure to the Head with backstitches all around the edges.

3. For Boy: Position the Hair in the center of the Face, and sew in place with backstitches around the edges.

HOOD

Note: *Before making the Hood, the Head must be finished – with the facial features complete, and the Hair attached.*

Rounds 1-23: Using **Color E** (for Girl) or **Color H**
(for Boy), repeat Rounds 1-23 of Head.

Rounds 24-26: *(3 rounds)* Sc in each st around. (72)

Place the finished Head in the Hood. (The following decrease rounds of the Hood will then "fit" nicely around the Head.) *(image 9-10)*

Round 27: [Inv-dec, sc in each of next 10 sts] 6 times. (66 sc)
(image 11-12)

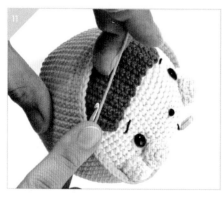

Round 28: [Inv-dec, sc in each of next 9 sts] 6 times. (60 sc)

Last Row: Inv-dec, sc in each of the next 8 sts, inv-dec (10 sc) Leave remaining sts unworked. Fasten off with a Needle Join, leaving a long tail for sewing.

BEAR EARS – for Girl (Make 2)

Round 1: With **Color E**, make a magic ring, 6 sc in ring. (6 sc)

Round 2: Inc in each st around. (12 sc)

Round 3: [Inc in next st, sc in next st] 6 times. (18 sc)

Rounds 4-6: *(3 rounds)* Sc in each st around. (18 sc)
At the end of Round 6, fasten off, leaving a long tail for sewing.

BUNNY EARS – for Boy (Make 2)

Round 1: With **Color H**, make a magic ring, 6 sc in ring. (6 sc)

Round 2: Inc in each st around. (12 sc)

Rounds 3-10: *(8 rounds)* Sc in each st around. (12 sc)
At the end of Round 10, fasten off, leaving a long tail for sewing.

BODY

Round 1: Using **Color E** (for Girl) or **Color H** (for Boy), make a magic ring, 6 sc in ring. (6 sc)

Round 2: Inc in each st around. (12 sc)

Round 3: [Inc in next st, sc in next st] 6 times. (18 sc)

Round 4: [Inc in next st, sc in each of next 2 sts] 6 times. (24 sc)

Round 5: [Inc in next st, sc in each of next 3 sts] 6 times. (30 sc)

Round 6: [Inc in next st, sc in each of next 4 sts] 6 times. (36 sc)

Round 7: [Inc in next st, sc in each of next 5 sts] 6 times. (42 sc)

Round 8: [Inc in next st, sc in each of next 6 sts] 6 times. (48 sc)

Round 9: [Inc in next st, sc in each of next 7 sts] 6 times. (54 sc)

Round 10: [Inc in next st, sc in each of next 8 sts] 6 times. (60 sc)

Rounds 11-21: *(11 rounds)* Sc in each st around. (60 sc)

Round 22: [Inv-dec, sc in each of next 8 sts] 6 times. (54 sc)

Round 23: [Inv-dec, sc in each of next 7 sts] 6 times. (48 sc)

Round 24: [Inv-dec, sc in each of next 6 sts] 6 times. (42 sc) Fasten off, leaving a long tail for sewing.

Stuff body firmly. (**Optional stuffing method:** Place stuffing beads in a stocking and knot securely. Place the stuffed pouch in the base of body, then add the regular stuffing.) *(image 13)*

ARM (Make 2)

Round 1: With **MC**, make a magic ring, 6 sc in ring. (6 sc)

Round 2: Inc in each st around. (12 sc)

Rounds 3-4: *(2 rounds)* Sc in each st around. (12 sc)
At the end of Round 4, change to **Color E** (for Girl) or **Color H** (for Boy).

Rounds 5-15: *(11 rounds)* Sc in each st around. (12 sc)
At the end of Round 15, fasten off, leaving a long tail for sewing.

Stuff the Hand lightly – not the whole Arm.

LEG (Make 2)

Round 1: With **Color D**, make a magic ring, 6 sc in ring. (6 sc)

Round 2: Inc in each st around. (12 sc) Change to **Color A**.

Round 3: [Inc in next st, sc in next st] 6 times. (18 sc)

Round 4: [Inc in next st, sc in each of next 2 sts] 6 times. (24 sc) Change to **Color E** (for Girl) or **Color H** (for Boy).

Round 5: Working in **back loops** only, [inc in next st, sc in each of next 3 sts] 6 times. (30 sc)

Round 6: [Inv-dec] 3 times, sc in each of the next 24 sts. (27 sc)

Round 7: [Inv-dec] 3 times, sc in each of the next 21 sts. (24 sc)

Round 8: [Inv-dec] 3 times, sc in each of the next 18 sts. (21 sc)

Rounds 9-14: *(6 rounds)* Sc in each st around. (21 sc)
At the end of Round 14, fasten off, leaving a long tail for sewing. Stuff the Foot lightly – not the whole Leg.

FINISHING THE LEGS

Paw Pads

Cut a strand of **Color D**, and using the yarn needle, bring the yarn up from the inside of the Leg between Round 3 and Round 4 (Color A part of Foot). Make 3 French Knots next to each other, wrapping the yarn 4 times around the needle for each knot. Take the yarn back inside the Leg and tie the ends together to secure.

Repeat on other Leg. *(image 14-17)*

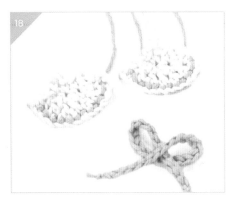

COLLAR (Make 2)

Row 1: With **Color A**, ch 15, starting in 2nd ch from hook, [dec] 7 times across. (7 sc)

Row 2: Ch 1, turn, [dec] 3 times, sc in the last st. (4 sc)

Row 3: Ch 1, turn, sc in each st across. (4 sc) Fasten off, leaving a long tail for sewing.

Using a strand of **Color D**, embroider backstitches near the edge on both pieces to add on a pretty border. *(image 18)*

ACCESSORIES

CHERRY (Make 2)

Round 1: With **Color F**, make a magic ring, 3 sc in ring. (3 sc) Tug tail to tighten ring. Fasten off with a Needle Join, leaving a long tail for sewing.

Hint: Push the center out, so it will look like a cherry when sewn on. (image 19)

BOWTIE

With **Color D**, ch 30. Fasten off securely and trim both ends neatly.

Bowtie Center

Round 1: With **Color D**, make a magic ring, 3 sc in ring. (3 sc) Tug tail to tighten ring. Fasten off with a Needle Join, leaving a long tail for sewing.

Hint: Push the center out, so it forms a bump (like the cherry). (image 20)

DOLL ASSEMBLY

1. Flatten each Ear. Position the Ears on Round 24 of the Hood and sew in place. The Girl's Bear Ears have about 6 stitches between them, and the Boy's Bunny Ears have about 2 stitches between them. The Bunny Ears can be bent slightly to make them cuter. *(image 21)*

2. Pin the rest of the pieces in position before sewing. *(image 22-23)*

3. Sew the Body to the finished Head, adding more stuffing before finishing.

4. Position the Collar pieces side-by-side and sew to the Body with backstitches across the top edge only.

5. Position the Arms and sew in place.

6. Position the Legs at Round 12 of the Body, so the doll can sit well. Sew in place.

7. Position the Cherries about 3-4 rounds below the Collar, with about 2 stitches between them, and sew to the Body. Using **Color G**, embroider Leaves with about four long horizontal straight stitches, and Stems with diagonal backstitches.

8. For the Bowtie, shape the chain length into a bow-shape. Position the Bow below the Collar and sew the Bowtie Center through the middle of the Bow to secure the Bow to the Body.

maya
The Bunny

designer

Elisa Ems Domenig
@lululovesthemoon

Materials & Tools

HELLO Cotton Yarn

For Bunny
- » **Color A:** Dark Beige (158)
- » **Color B:** Mocha (125) - for Head Bow

Overalls
- » **Color C:** Mint Green (138)
- » **Small amounts of:** Orange (119), Gray (159) & Light Pink (102) for Rainbow.

Dress
- » **Color D:** Sea Green (136)

Hook Size
- » 2.25 mm hook - for Bunny
- » 2.5 mm hook - for Clothes

Other
- » Stitch Markers
- » Yarn Needle
- » Stuffing
- » DMC Embroidery Floss - Black & White (Eyes & Eyebrows) & Light Pink (Nose)
- » Embroidery Needle
- » Cosmetic Blusher – Pink (Cheeks) & Light Brown (Ears)
- » Small Button (for Dress)
- » Sewing thread and needle

Finished Size
Bunny – About 12½″ (32 cm) tall
(including Ears)
Overalls – About 6½″ (17 cm) long
Dress – About 4½″ (11 cm) long

Skill Level
Bunny - Easy
Clothes - Intermediate

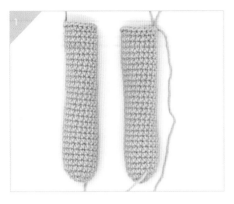

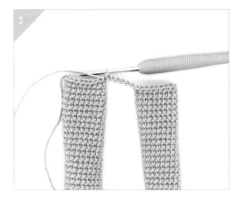

BUNNY

HEAD

Round 1: With **Color A** and smaller hook, make a magic ring, 6 sc in ring. (6 sc) Do not join. Mark last st. Move marker at the end of each round.

Round 2: Inc in each sc around. (12 sc)

Round 3: [Sc in next sc, inc in next sc] around. (18 sc)

Round 4: [Sc in each of next 2 sc, inc in next sc] around. (24 sc)

Round 5: [Sc in each of next 3 sc, inc in next sc] around. (30 sc)

Round 6: [Sc in each of next 4 sc, inc in next sc] around. (36 sc)

Round 7: [Sc in each of next 5 sc, inc in next sc] around. (42 sc)

Round 8: [Sc in each of next 6 sc, inc in next sc] around. (48 sc)

Round 9: [Sc in each of next 7 sc, inc in next sc] around. (54 sc)

Round 10: [Sc in each of next 8 sc, inc in next sc] around. (60 sc)

Round 11: [Sc in each of next 9 sc, inc in next sc] around. (66 sc)

Round 12: [Sc in each of next 10 sc, inc in next sc] around. (72 sc)

Rounds 13-25: *(13 rounds)* Sc in each sc around. (72 sc)

Round 26: [Sc in each of next 10 sc, dec] around. (66 sc)

Round 27: [Sc in each of next 9 sc, dec] around. (60 sc)

Round 28: [Sc in each of next 8 sc, dec] around. (54 sc)

Round 29: [Sc in each of next 7 sc, dec] around. (48 sc)

Round 30: [Sc in each of next 6 sc, dec] around. (42 sc)

Start stuffing Head firmly, adding more as you go.

Round 31: [Sc in each of next 5 sc, dec] around. (36 sc)

Round 32: [Sc in each of next 4 sc, dec] around. (30 sc)

Round 33: [Sc in each of next 3 sc, dec] around. (24 sc)

Fasten off, leaving a long tail for sewing. Do not close the neck opening.

Finish stuffing Head.

BODY

Leg (Make 2)

Rounds 1-3: With **Color A** and smaller hook, repeat Rounds 1-3 of Head.

Rounds 4-29: *(26 rounds)* Sc in each sc around. (18 sc)

Start stuffing Leg firmly, adding more as you go.

At the end of Round 29, for the First Leg, fasten off and weave in ends. For the Second Leg, do not fasten off. Continue with Body. *(image 1 - image 2)*

Body

Round 1: *(Joining Legs)* Ch 6, working on First Leg, sc in any st, *(image 3).*, sc in each of next 17 sc; working in starting ch-6, sc in each of next 6 ch; working on Second Leg, sc in each of next 18 sc; working on other side of starting chain, sc in each of next 6 ch. (48 sc) Mark last stitch. Move marker each round.

Rounds 2-12: *(11 rounds)* Sc in each sc around. (48 sc)

Round 13: [Sc in each of next 6 sc, dec] around. (42 sc)

Rounds 14-15: *(2 rounds)* Sc in each sc around. (42 sc)

Round 16: [Sc in each of next 5 sc, dec] around. (36 sc)

Start stuffing Body firmly, adding more as you go.

Rounds 17-18: *(2 rounds)* Sc in each sc around. (36 sc)

Round 19: [Sc in each of next 4 sc, dec] around. (30 sc)

Rounds 20-21: *(2 rounds)* Sc in each sc around. (30 sc)

Round 22: [Sc in each of next 3 sc, dec] around. (24 sc)

Rounds 23-24: *(2 rounds)* Sc in each sc around. (24 sc) Fasten off, leaving a long tail for sewing. Do not close neck opening.

Finish stuffing Body.

Using long tail from Head and yarn needle, position Head to Body and then matching stitches, sew in place, adding more stuffing to make the neck very firm.

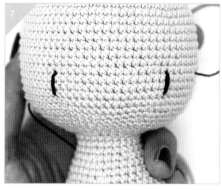
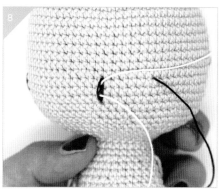

EAR (Make 2)

Note: *Do not stuff Ears.*

Round 1: With **Color A** and smaller hook, make a magic ring, 6 sc in ring. (6 sc) Do not join. Mark last st. Move marker at the end of each round.

Round 2: Sc in each sc around. (6 sc)

Round 3: Inc in each sc around. (12 sc)

Round 4: Sc in each sc around. (12 sc)

Round 5: [Sc in next sc, inc in next sc] around. (18 sc)

Round 6: [Sc in each of next 5 sc, inc in next sc] around. (21 sc)

Rounds 7-15: *(9 rounds)* Sc in each sc around. (21 sc)

Round 16: [Sc in each of next 5 sc, dec] around. (18 sc)

Round 17: [Sc in next sc, dec] around. (12 sc) Fasten off, leaving a long tail for sewing. *(image 4)*.

Fold each flattened Ear down the middle, and from fold, sew 1-2 stitches together. *(image 5)*.

Position Ears on top of Head, and using yarn tails, sew in place. *(image 6)*.

ARM (Make 2)

Note: *Do not stuff Arms.*

Rounds 1-2: With **Color A** and smaller hook, repeat Rounds 1-2 of Head.

Rounds 3-20: *(18 rounds)* Sc in each sc around. (12 sc)

Last Row: Flatten Arm, working through both thicknesses,

sc in each of next 5 sts. Fasten off, leaving a long tail for sewing.

Position Arms directly under Head, and using yarn tails, sew in place.

FINISHING THE FACE

Eyes

- Using Black Floss, embroider Eyes between Rounds 21-25 of Head (with 15 stitches between the Eyes), using straight vertical stitches.

- Using White Floss, embroider the whites of the Eyes in the center of Eye using small straight stitches. *(image 7 - image 8)*.

Nose

- Using Pink Floss, embroider a Nose at Round 24, between the Eyes.

Eyebrows

- Black Floss, embroider a diagonal stitch, 6 rounds above each Eye.

Cheeks and Ears

- With a small make-up brush, apply pink Blusher to the Cheeks, and brown Blusher inside the Ears. *(image 9)*.

CLOTHES

OVERALLS

Pants Leg (Make 2)

Round 1: With **Color C** and larger hook, ch 22; join with a sl st to the first ch to form a ring *(image 10)*; ch 1, sc in each ch around. (22 sc) Do not join. Mark last st. Move marker at the end of each round.

Rounds 2-18: *(17 rounds)* Sc in each sc around. (22 sc)

At the end of Round 18, for the First Pants Leg, fasten off and weave in ends *(image 11)*. For the Second Pants Leg, do not fasten off *(image 12)*. Continue with Pants.

Pants

Round 1: *(Joining Pants Legs)* Ch 4, working on First Pants Leg, sc in any st, *(image 13)* sc in each of next 21 sc; working in starting ch-4, sc in each of next 4 ch; working on Second Pants Leg, sc in each of next 22 sc; working on other side of starting chain, sc in each of next 4 ch. (52 sc) Mark last stitch. Move marker each round.

Round 2: Sc in each sc around. (52 sc)

Round 3: [Sc in each of next 11 sc, dec] around. (48 sc)

Round 4: Sc in each sc around. (48 sc)

Round 5: [Sc in each of next 10 sc, dec] around. (44 sc)

Round 6: Sc in each sc around. (44 sc)

Round 7: [Sc in each of next 9 sc, dec] around. (40 sc)

Round 8: [Sc in each of next 8 sc, dec] around. (36 sc)

Round 9: Sc in each of next 26 sc. (26 sc)

Note: Check if the last sc is in the side of Pants, you may need to work a few less or more sc. Finish Round 9 here and do not work the rest of 10 sc.

Fasten off and weave in ends. *(image 14)*

Mark the 10 stitches at center front of Pants (for Bib).

Mark the 13 stitches at center back (for attaching Straps).

Pants Bib

Row 1: Attach **Color C** to first marked st on Pants front *(image 15)*, ch 1, sc in same st, sc in each of next 9 sts. *(image 16)* (10 sc)

Rows 2-8: *(7 rows)* Ch 1, turn, sc in each st across. (10 sc)

At the end of Row 8, do not fasten off. Continue with Bib Straps.

- Place Bunny in Overalls. *(image 17)*.

Bib Straps

Ch 25; wrap the chain over the Bunny shoulder to the opposite side, sl st in first marked st at back, sc in each of next 11 sc, sl st in next marked st, ch 25, wrap the chain over the opposite shoulder *(crossing the straps at the back)*, sl st in first st of Row 8 on Bib. Fasten off and weave in ends. *(images 18-22)*

- Take Overalls off Bunny.

Bib Ruffle

Row 1: Attach **Color C** to same marked stitch where Bib started, *(image 23)*; working in sides of rows, ch 1, inc in each row across. (16 sc)

Row 2: Ch 1, turn, inc in each st across. (32 sc) Fasten off and weave in ends.

Repeat Bib Ruffle on other side, starting at same stitch as last sl st (1st st of Row 8).

Using 3 different colors, embroider a Rainbow (back-stitches) to the front of the Bib. *(image 24 - image 25)*.

DRESS

Note: *The skipped chs in Row 1 and the turning ch-2 stitches do not count as first stitch.*

Row 1: (Right Side) With **Color D** and larger hook, ch 28, starting in 3rd ch from hook, [dc in next ch, 2 dc in next ch] across. (39 dc)

Row 2: Ch 2, turn, dc in first st, [2 dc in next dc, dc in next dc] across. (58 dc) *(image 26)*

Work continues in Rounds.

Round 1: Ch 1, turn, sc in same st, sc in each of next 6 sts, ch 3, skip next 12 sts, *(armhole)*, sc in each of next 18 sts, ch 3, skip next 12 sts, sc in each of next 5 sts. Leave the remaining 4 sts unworked; join with a sl st to first sc. (30 sc & 2 ch-3 lps) *(image 27 - image 28)*

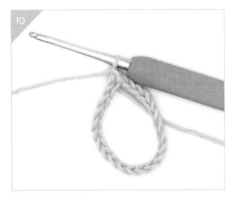

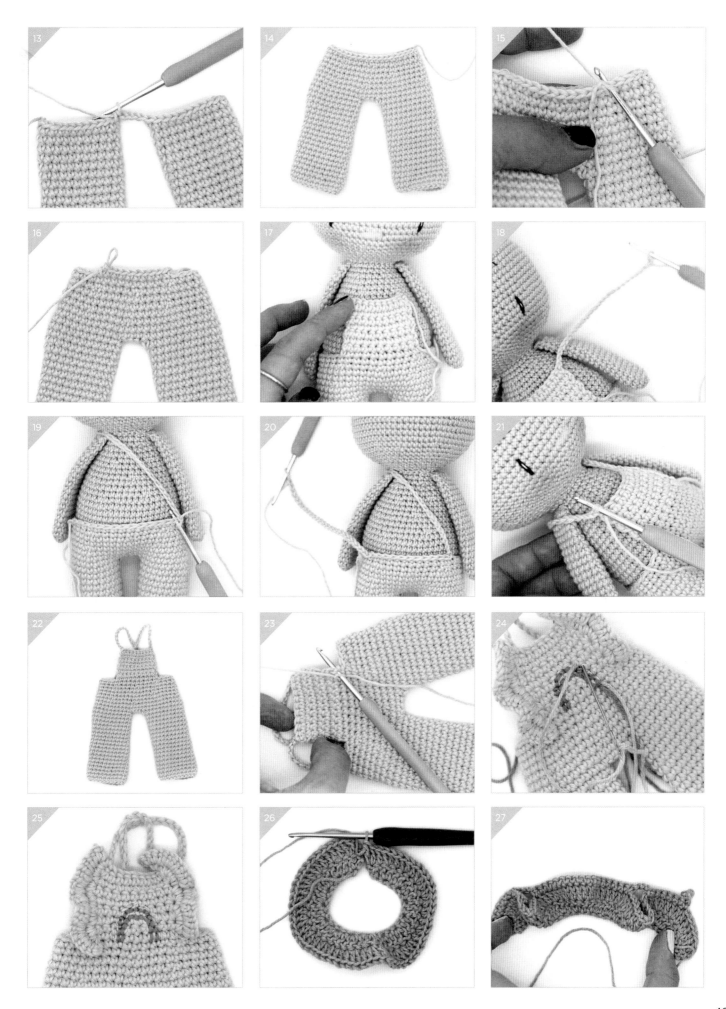

Round 2: Ch 1, inc in each of next 7 sts, inc in each of next 3 chs, inc in each of next 18 sts, inc in each of next 3 chs, inc in each of next 5 sts; join with sl st to first sc. (72 sc)

Rounds 3-10: *(8 rounds)* Ch 2, dc in each st around; join with sl st to first dc. (72 dc) Fasten off, weaving in ends.

Dress Collar

Row 1: With right side of upside down Dress facing, working on other side of starting ch-28, attach **Color D** to first ch *(image 29)*, ch 1, 2 dc in same ch, 2 dc in each of next 24 ch. (50 dc) Leave remaining ch-sts unworked.

Row 2: Ch 2, turn, dc in first st, 2 dc in next st, [dc in next st, 2 dc in next st] across. (75 dc)

Row 3: Ch 2, turn, dc in each st across. (75 dc) Fasten off and weave in ends. *(image 30)*

Sew Button to the back of Dress, using a hole between the stitches as a buttonhole. *(image 31)*

HEAD BOW

Round 1: With **Color B** and larger hook, ch 20; join with a sl st to first ch to form a ring; ch1, sc in each ch around. (20 sc) Do not join. Mark last st. Move marker at the end of each round.

Rounds 2-3: *(2 rounds)* Sc in each sc around. (20 sc)

At the end of Round 3, fasten off, leaving a long tail.

Wrap the long tail tightly around the center of the Bow and secure it firmly, leaving a long tail for sewing onto Strap. *(image 32)*

Head Strap

With **Color B**, ch 90. Fasten off and trim the tails on both ends.

Place Head Bow on Head, and tie in place.

Cowgirl

designer

Gülizar Sezer

@amigurumibyguli

Materials & Tools

HELLO Cotton Yarn

» **Main Color (MC)** - Beige (157) - for Body

» **Color A:** Sage (137) - for Shirt & Hobby Horse Mane

» **Color B:** Brick Red (117) - for Boots & Hat

» **Color C:** Sky Blue (147) - for Skirt & Hair Ties

» **Color D:** Mustard (124) - for Hair & Hobby Horse Halter

» **Color E:** Mocha (125) - for Vest & Hobby Horse pole

» **Color F:** Lilac (139) - for Bandanna & Hobby Horse

Hook Size

» 2.25 mm hook

Other

» Stitch Markers

» Yarn Needle

» Stuffing

» Straight Pins

» Safety Eyes - Black Round (6 mm) x 2

» Strong Cotton Thread - for Eye indents.

» DMC Embroidery Floss – Black & White – for facial features

» Embroidery Needle

» Copper Electronic Wire – for Hobby Horse Pole

Finished Size

About 9″ (23 cm) tall

Skill Level

Intermediate

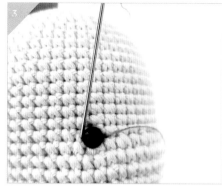
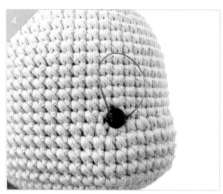

DOLL

HEAD

Round 1: With **MC**, make a magic ring; ch 1, 8 sc in ring. (8 sc) Tug tail to tighten ring. Do not join. Mark last st. Move marker at the end of each round.

Round 2: Inc in each st around. (16 sc)

Round 3: [Sc in next st, inc in next st] 8 times. (24 sc)

Round 4: [Sc in each of next 3 sts, inc in next st] 6 times. (30 sc)

Round 5 [Sc in each of next 4 sts, inc in next st] 6 times. (36 sc)

Round 6: [Sc in each of next 5 sts, inc in next st] 6 times. (42 sc)

Round 7: [Sc in each of next 6 sts, inc in next st] 6 times. (48 sc)

Round 8: [Sc in each of next 7 sts, inc in next st] 6 times. (54 sc)

Rounds 9-18: *(10 Rounds)* Sc in each st around. (54 sc)

Round 19: Sc in each of next 12 sts, [sc in next st, inc in next st] 5 times, sc in each of next 10 sts *(mark these 10 sts as they must be between the Eyes)*, [sc in next st, inc in next st] 5 times, sc in each of next 12 sts (64 sc)

Rounds 20-23: *(4 Rounds)* Sc in each st around. (64 sc)

Round 24: Sc in each of next 12 sts, [sc in next st, dec] 5 times, sc in each of next 10 sts, [sc in next st, dec] 5 times, sc in each of next 12 sts (54 sc)

- Insert Safety Eyes between Rounds 18 & 19, about 12 stitches apart – with the 10 marked stitches between them. *(image 1)*

Round 25: [Sc in each of next 7 sts, dec] 6 times. (48 sc)

Round 26: [Sc in each of next 6 sts, dec] 6 times. (42 sc)

Round 27: [Sc in each of next 5 sts, dec] 6 times. (36 sc)

Round 28: [Sc in each of next 4 sts, dec] 6 times. (30 sc) Stuff Head firmly, adding more as you go.

Round 29: [Sc in each of next 3 sts, dec] 6 times. (24 sc)

Round 30: [Sc in each of next 2 sts, dec] 6 times. (18 sc) Fasten off, leaving a long tail for sewing.

FINISHING THE FACE

1. Using a long strand of the strong Cotton Thread, bring the needle up through the bottom of the Head and out on the side of one Eye. Insert the needle on the other side of the Eye, bringing it out next to the other Eye. Insert the needle down on the other side of that Eye, bringing it out at the bottom of the Head. Tug the two strand ends firmly to shape the eye sockets. Knot the strands together to secure. *(images 2-3-4-5)*

2. Using photos as guide, with White Floss, embroider Eye highlights, and with the Black Floss, embroider Eyelashes on both Eyes, and a Mouth – using a loose straight stitch and then shaping the Mouth with two small vertical stitches. *(images 6,7 & 8)*

3. With MC, embroider a Nose, using horizontal straight stitches. *(image 9)*

ARM (Make 2)

Note: *Arms are not stuffed.*

Round 1: With **MC**, make a magic ring; ch 1, 6 sc in ring. (6 sc) Tug tail to tighten ring. Do not join. Mark last st. Move marker at the end of each round.

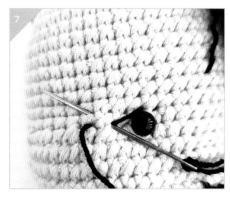

Round 2: Inc in each st around. (12 sc)

Rounds 3-4: *(2 Rounds)* Sc in each st around. (12 sc)

Round 5: [Sc in each of next 4 sts, dec] 2 times. (10 sc)

At the end of Round 5, change to **Color C.** Fasten off MC.

Rounds 6-15: *(10 Rounds)* Sc in each st around. (10 sc)

Round 16: Sc in each of next 8 sts, dec. (9 sc)

Round 17: Sc in each st around. (9 sc)

Round 18: Sc in each of next 7 sts, dec. (8 sc)

Last Row: Flatten Arm, working through both thicknesses, sc in each of next 4 sts. (4 sc) Fasten off. *(image 10-11)*

BODY

Legs

First Leg

Round 1: With **Color B**, make a magic ring; ch 1, 6 sc in ring, DO NOT JOIN. (6 sc) Tug tail to tighten ring. Mark last stitch, move the marker each round.

Round 2: [Sc in next st, inc in next st] 3 times. (9 sc)

Round 3: [Sc in each of next 2 sts, inc in next st] 3 times. (12 sc)

Round 4: Sc in each st around. (12 sc)

Round 5: [Sc in each of next 5 sts, inc in next st] 2 times. (14 sc)

Rounds 6-7: *(2 Rounds)* Sc in each st around. (14 sc) At the end of Round 7, change to **MC.** Fasten off Color B.

Round 8: Working in **back loops** only, sc in each st around. (14 sc)

Round 9: [inc in next st, Sc in each of next 13 sts] (15 sc)

Round 10: Sc in each st around. (15 sc)

Round 11: [inc in next st, Sc in each of next 14 sts] (16 sc)

Round 12: Sc in each st around. (16 sc)

Round 13: [Sc in next st, inc in next st, Sc in each of next 14 sts] (17 sc)

Round 14: Sc in each st around. (17 sc) Fasten off.

Second Leg

Rounds 1-8: Repeat Rounds 1-8 of First Leg.

Round 9: [Sc in each of next 7 sts, inc in next st, Sc in each of next 6 sts] (15 sc)

Round 10: Sc in each st around. (15 sc)

Round 11: [Sc in each of next 8 sts, inc in next st, Sc in each of next 6 sts] (16 sc)

Round 12: Sc in each st around. (16 sc)

Round 13: [Sc in each of next 9 sts, inc in next st, Sc in each of next 6 sts] (17 sc)

Round 14: Sc in each st around. (17 sc) Do not fasten off.

Body

Round 1: *(Joining Legs)* Ch 3; working on First Leg, sc in 12th st made *(image 12)*, sc in each of next 7 sts, inc in next st, sc in each of next 8 sts; working in ch-3, sc in each of next 3 ch; working on Second Leg, sc in each of next 8 sts, inc in next st, sc in each of next 8 sts; working on other side of ch-3, sc in each of next 3 ch. (42 sc) Mark last st made. Move marker each round.

Rounds 2-3: *(2 Rounds)* Sc in each st around. (42 sc)

Round 4: [Sc in each of next 8 sts, dec, sc in each of next 19 sts, dec, sc in each of next 11 sts] (40 sc)

Round 5: Sc in each st around. (40 sc)

Round 6: [Sc in each of next 8 sts, dec, sc in each of next 18 sts, dec, sc in each of next 10 sts] (38 sc)

At the end of Round 6, change to **Color A.** Fasten off MC.

Round 7: Sc in each st around. (38 sc)

Round 8: Working in **back loops** only, sc in each st around. (38 sc)

- Start stuffing Legs and Body, adding more as you go.

Round 9: [Sc in each of next 7 sts, dec, sc in each of next 17 sts, dec, sc in each of next 10 sts] (36 sc)

Round 10: Sc in each st around. (36 sc)

Round 11: [Sc in each of next 7 sts, dec, sc in each of next 16 sts, dec, sc in each of next 9 sts] (34 sc)

Round 12: Sc in each st around. (34 sc)

Round 13: [Sc in each of next 6 sts, dec, sc in each of next 16 sts, dec, sc in each of next 8 sts] (32 sc)

Rounds 14-15: *(2 Rounds)* Sc in each st around. (32 sc)

Round 16: [Sc in each of next 6 sts, dec, sc in each of next 14 sts, dec, sc in each of next 8 sts] (30 sc)

Round 17: Sc in each st around. (30 sc)

Round 18: [Sc in each of next 3 sts, dec] 6 times. (24 sc)

Round 19: Sc in each st around. (24 sc)

Round 20: *(Joining Arms)* Sc in each of next 4 sts; working through both thicknesses *(Last Row of one Arm & Body),* sc in each of the next 4 sts; working on Body only, sc in each of the next 7 sts; working through both thicknesses *(Last Row of other Arm & Body),* sc in each of the next 4 sts; working on Body only, sc in each of next 5 sts. (24sc) *(image 13)*

Round 21: Sc in each st around. (24 sc)

Round 22: [Sc in each of next 2 sts, dec] 6 times. (18 sc)

Rounds 23-25: *(3 Rounds)* Sc in each st around. (18 sc) *(image 14)* Fasten off, leaving a long tail for sewing.

- Add more stuffing to Head and Neck.

- Place Head over Neck and using yarn tails, sew Head to Body between Rounds 23 & 24. *(image 15)*

SKIRT

Round 1: Holding the Doll upside down, working in unused front loops of Round 7 on Body, join **Color C** to st at center back *(image 16),* ch 1, sc in each st around; join with sl st to first sc. (38 sc) *(image 17)* Join all rounds in this manner.

Round 2: Ch 1, [sc in next st, inc in next st] 19 times; join. (57 sc)

Round 3: Ch 1, sc in each st around; join. (57 sc)

Round 4: Ch 1, sc in each of next 9 sts, [inc in next st, sc in each of next 18 sts] 2 times, inc in next st, sc in each of next 9 sts (60 sc)

Rounds 5-7: *(3 Rounds)* Sc in each st around. (60 sc)

Round 8: *(Ruffle)* [Skip next 2 sts, 5 dc in next sts, skip next 2 sts, sl st in next st] 10 times. Fasten off and weave in ends. *(image 18)*

SHOE DETAIL

Round 1: Holding the Doll upside down, working in unused front loops of Round 7 on Legs, join **Color B** to the st at center back *(image 19)*; ch 2, [dc in each of next 2 sts, 2 dc in next st] 4 times, dc in each of next 2 sts; join with sl st to first dc. (18 dc) *(image 20)* Fasten off and weave in all ends.

HAT

Note: Hat is worked in joined rounds.

Round 1: With **Color B**, make a magic ring; ch 1, 12 sc in ring *(tug tail to tighten ring)*; join with sl st to first sc. (12 sc) Join all rounds in this manner.

Round 2: Ch 1, inc in each st around; join. (24 sc)

Round 3: Ch 1, sc in each of next 3 sts, inc in each of next 6 sts, sc in each of next 6 sts, inc in each of next 6 sts, sc in each of next 3 sts; join. (36 sc)

Round 4: Ch 1, sc in each of next 6 sts, inc in each of next 6 sts, sc in each of next 12 sts, inc in each of next 6 sts, sc in each of next 6 sts; join. (48 sc)

Round 5 Ch 1, [sc in each of next 7 sts, inc next st] 6 times; join. (54 sc)

Round 6: Ch 1, sc in each st around; join. (54 sc)

Round 7: Ch 1, [sc in each of next 17 sts, inc in next st] 3 times; join. (57 sc)

Round 8: Ch 1, sc in each st around; join. (57 sc)

Round 9: Ch 1, sc in each of next 9 sts, [inc in next st, sc in each of next 18 sts] 2 times, inc in next st, sc in each of next 9 sts; join. (60 sc)

Round 10: Ch 1, sc in each st around; join. (60 sc)

Round 11: Ch 1, [sc in each of next 19 sts, inc in next st] 3 times; join. (63 sc)

Round 12: Ch 1, sc in each st around. (63 sc)

Round 13: Ch 1, sc in each of next 10 sts, [inc in next st, sc in each of next 20 sts] 2 times, inc in next st, sc in each of next 10 sts; join. (66 sc)

Rounds 14-15: *(2 Rounds)* Ch 1, sc in each st around; join. (66 sc)

Round 16: Ch 1, [sc in each of next 21 sts, inc in next st] 3 times; join. (69 sc)

Rounds 17-18: *(2 Rounds)* Ch 1, sc in each st around; join. (69 sc)

Round 19: Ch 1, sc in each of next 11 sts, [inc in next st, sc in each of next 22 sts] 2 times, inc in next st, sc in each of next 11 sts; join. (72 sc)

Rounds 20-21: *(2 Rounds)* Ch 1, sc in each st around; join. (72 sc)

Round 22: Ch 1, **turn**, sc in first st, inc in next st, [sc in next st, inc in next st] around; join. (108 sc) *(image 21)*

Round 23: Ch 1, [dec] 2 times, sc in each of next 46 sts, [dec] 4 times, sc in each of next 46 sts, [dec] 2 times; join. (100 sc)

Round 24: Ch 1, *dec, sc in each of next 20 sts, inc in next st, sc in next st, inc in each of next 2 sts, sc in next st, inc in next st, sc in each of next 20 sts, dec; repeat from * once more; join. (104 sc)

Round 25: Sc in each st around. (104 sc) Fasten off and weave in ends. *(image 22)*

HAIR

Round 1: With **Color D**, make a magic ring; ch 1, 8 sc in ring (8 sc) Tug tail to tighten ring. Do not join. Mark last st. Move marker at the end of each round.

Round 2: Inc in each st around. (16 sc)

Round 3: [Sc in next st, inc in next st] 8 times. (24 sc)

Round 4: [Sc in each of next 3 sts, inc in next st] 6 times. (30 sc)

Round 5: [Sc in each of next 4 sts, inc in next st] 6 times. (36 sc)

Round 6: [Sc in each of next 5 sts, inc in next st] 6 times. (42 sc)

Round 7: [Sc in each of next 6 sts, inc in next st] 6 times. (48 sc)

Round 8: Sc in each st around. (48 sc)

Round 9: [Sc in each of next 7 sts, inc in next st] 6 times. (54 sc)

Round 10: Sc in each st around. (54 sc)

Round 11: [Sc in each of next 17 sts, inc in next st] 3 times. (57 sc)

Round 12: Sc in each of next 9 sts, [inc in next st, sc in each of next 18 sts] 2 times, inc in next st, sc in each of next 9 sts (60 sc)

Round 13: Sc in each st around. (60 sc)

Round 14: [Sc in each of next 19 sts, inc in next st] 3 times. (63 sc)

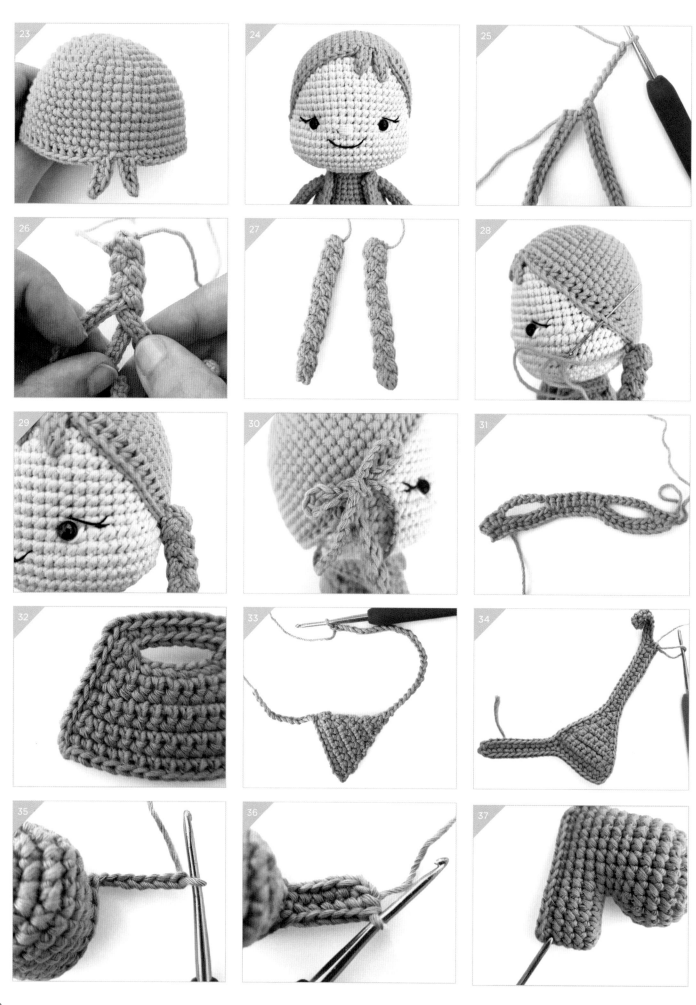

Rounds 15-17: *(3 Rounds)* Sc in each st around. (63 sc)

Round 18: Sc in each of next 10 sts, hdc in each of next 15 sts, sc in next st, *ch 5, starting in 2nd ch from hook, sc in each ch across *(4 sc)*, sl st in each of next 2 sts; repeat from * to * once, sc in next st, hdc in each of next 24 sts, sc in each of next 10 sts. *(image 23)* Fasten off, leaving a long tail for sewing.

Position Hair on Head with straight pins. Using tail and yarn needle, sew in place. *(images 24)*

Hair Braids (Make 2)

With **Color D**, [ch 26, starting in 2nd ch from hook, sc in each ch across *(25 sc)*] 3 times. (3 strands of 25 sc each) Fasten off, leaving a long tail for sewing. *(image 25)*

On each piece, braid the three Hair strands together. Using a strand of **Color D** and a yarn needle, sew the ends to secure the Braids. *(image 26-27)*

Position the Braids on either side of the Head and sew in place. *(image 28-29)*

Hair Ties (Make 2)

With **Color C**, ch 60. Fasten off, and trim the ends. Wrap a Tie around each Braid and make into a Bow. *(image 30)*

VEST

Row 1: With **Color E**, ch 25, starting in 2nd ch from hook, sc in each ch across. (24 sc).

Row 2: Ch 1, turn, sc in first st, inc in next st, ch 7, skip next 7 sts, inc in next st, sc in each of next 4 sts, inc in next st, ch 7, skip next 7 sts, inc in next st, sc in last st. (14 sc & 2 ch-7 lps) *(image 31)*

Row 3: Ch 1, turn, sc in each of first 3 sts, working in ch-7, sc in each of next 7 ch; sc in each of next 8 sts, working in ch-7, sc in each of next 7 ch; sc in each of last 3 sts. (28 sc)

Row 4: Ch 1, turn, sc in each st across. (28 sc)

Row 5: Ch 1, turn, sc in first st, inc in next st, sc in each of next 7 sts, inc in next st, sc in each of next 8 sts, inc in next st, sc in each of next 7 sts, inc in next st, sc in last st. (32 sc)

Rows 6-7: *(2 rows)* Ch 1, turn, sc in each st across. (32 sc)

Row 8: Ch 1, turn, sc in first st, inc in next st, sc in each of next 28 sts, inc in next st, sc in last st. (34 sc)

Rows 9-10: *(2 rows)* Ch 1, turn, sc in each st across. (34 sc)

At the end of Row 10, mark last stitch.

Edging Round: Ch 1, turn, sl st evenly all around vest; join with sl st to marked stitch. Fasten off and weave in all ends. *(image 32)*

BANDANNA

Row 1: With **Color F**, ch 23, starting in 2nd ch from hook, sc in each of next 10 ch. Leave remaining ch-sts unworked. (10 sc)

Row 2: Ch 1, turn, dec *(using first 2 sts)*, sc in each of next 6 sts, dec *(using last 2 sts)*. (8 sc)

Row 3: Ch 1, turn, sc in each st across. (8 sc)

Row 4: Ch 1, turn, dec, sc in each of next 4 sts, dec. (6 sc)

Row 5: Ch 1, turn, sc in each st across. (6 sc)

Row 6: Ch 1, turn, [dec, sc in each of next 2 sts, dec. (4 sc)

Row 7: Ch 1, turn, sc in each st across. (4 sc)

Row 8: Ch 1, turn, [dec] 2 times. (2 sc)

Row 9: Ch 1, turn, sc in each st across. (2 sc)

Row 10: Ch 1, turn, dec *(using each st)*. (1 sc)

Row 11: Ch 1, turn, sc in only st. (1 sc)

Edging Round: Ch 26, starting in 2nd ch from hook, sc in each ch across; working in sides of rows of Scarf, sc in each row across, working in remaining ch-sts of ch-23, sc in each ch to end; working on other side of ch-23, sc in each ch across to next corner of Scarf; working in sides of rows, sc in each row across, working in ch-26, sc in each ch across to end. Fasten off and weave in ends. *(image 33-34)* Tie Scarf around neck of Doll.

HOBBY HORSE

Head

Round 1: With **Color F**, make a magic ring; ch 1, 6 sc in ring. (6 sc) Tug tail to tighten ring. Do not join. Mark last st. Move marker at the end of each round.

Round 2: Inc in each st around. (12 sc)

Round 3: [Sc in next st, inc in next st] 6 times. (18 sc)

Round 4: [Sc in each of next 2 sts, inc in next st] 6 times. (24 sc)

Rounds 5-6: *(2 rounds)* Sc in each st around. (24 sc)

Round 7: Dec, sc in each of next 20 sts, dec. (22 sc)

Round 8: Dec, sc in each of next 18 sts, dec. (20 sc)

Round 9: Dec, sc in each of next 16 sts, dec. (18 sc) Start stuffing Head firmly, adding more as you go.

Round 10: Ch 7, *(image 35)* starting in 2nd ch from hook, sc in each ch across *(6 sc)*, working in Rnd 9, sc in each of next 18 sts, working on other side of starting chain, sc in each of next 6 ch. (30 sc) *(image 36)* Move marker to last sc worked.

Rounds 11-14: *(4 rounds)* Sc in each st around. (30 sc) Finish stuffing Head.

Last Row: Flatten last round, working through both thicknesses, sc in each st across. (15 sc) Fasten off, weaving in ends.

Pole

Round 1: Attach **Color E**, to beginning of Last Row of Horse Head, *(image 37)*, work 8 sc between the stitches around in a circle. *(image 38-39)* (8 sc) Do not join. Mark last st. Move marker at the end of each round. *(image 40)*

Rounds 2-25: *(24 rounds)* Sc in each st around. (8 sc) *(image 41)*

At the end of Round 25, insert length of Copper Electronic Wire *(image 42-43)*. Fasten off, leaving long tail. Close the opening.

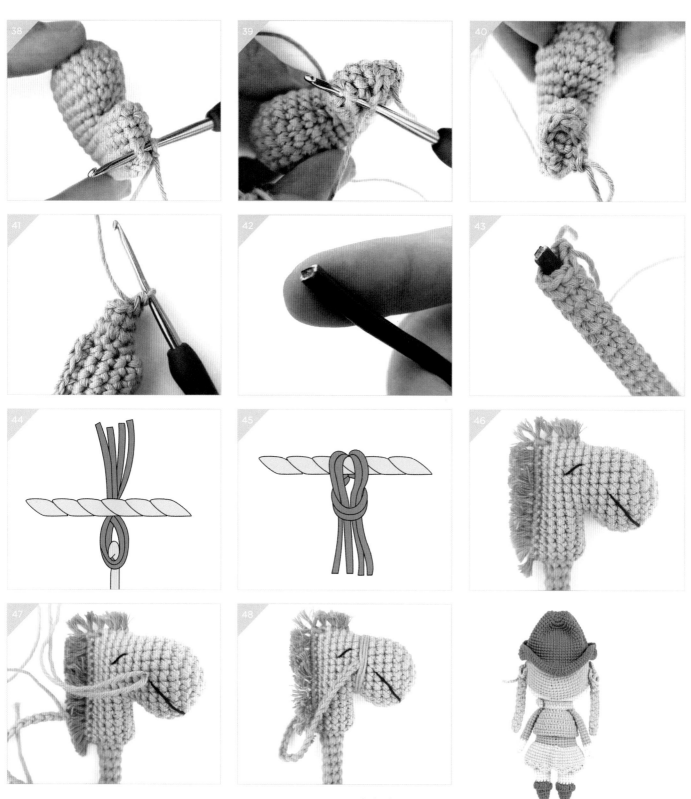

Horse Mane

Cut 20 strands of **Color A** – 2½" (6.5 cm) long.

The strands are attached along the Last Row and across top of Head, as follows:

Fold each strand in half. Insert hook under stitch and place folded end on hook. Pull the strand halfway through to form a loop. *(image 44-45)*

Then thread the strand tails through the loop and tug the tails to tighten.

Finishing Face

Using Black Floss, embroider an Eye on each side of the Head, using straight stitches. Embroider a Mouth, using backstitches. *(image 46)*

Horse Reins

With **Color D**, ch 36. Fasten off, leaving a long tail for sewing.

Using the tails and yarn needle, insert at either side of Head (as shown) *(image 47)*

Wrap the tails around the nose about 3 times. Secure the ends and fasten off. *(image 48)*

Candice

designer
Sandra Muller
@luciennecompotine

Materials & Tools

HELLO Cotton Yarn

For Doll

» **Main Color (MC):** Beige (157) - for Body
» **Color A:** White (154) - for Socks, Collar & Lollipop
» **Color B:** Light Pink (102) - for Dress & Bag Flower
» **Color C:** Off-White (155) - for Apron & Bag Flower
» **Color D:** Mustard (124) - for Hat
» **Color E:** Black (160) - for Shoes & Hat Band
» **Color F:** Mocha (125) - for Hair

Accessories

» **Color G:** Light Brown (128) - for Boho Bag
» **Color H:** Coral (111) - for Balloon & Lollipop

Hook Size

» 2.25 mm hook

Other

» Stitch Markers
» Yarn Needle
» Stuffing
» Straight Pins
» DMC Embroidery Floss - Black (for Eyes)
» Embroidery Needle
» Toothpick – for Lollipop
» **Optional:** 12″ long Chenille Wire (Pipe Cleaner) – for neck stability

---

Safety Note: This toy is not suitable for a child or infant when either the Wire is used in the Doll or a Toothpick is used with the Lollipop, as it could be a poking hazard. For a safer alternative, do not insert the Chenille Wire when making the Doll, and rather crochet a stick for the Lollipop.

Finished Size
About 11″ (27 cm) tall

Skill Level
Intermediate

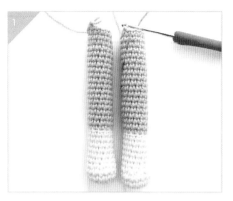
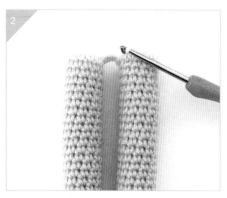
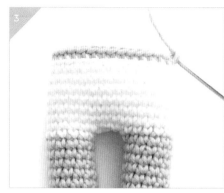
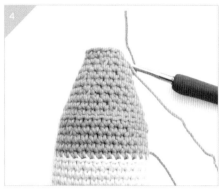

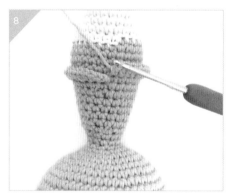

DOLL

BODY & HEAD

First Leg

Round 1: With **Color A**, make a magic ring, 7 sc in ring. (7 sc) Tug tail to close. Do not join. Mark last st. Move marker at the end of each round.

Round 2: Inc in each st around. (14 sc)

Rounds 3-4: (*2 rounds*) Sc in each st around. (14 sc)

Round 5: Sc in each of next 5 sts, [dec] twice, sc in each of next 5 sts. (12 sc)

Rounds 6-11: (*6 rounds*) Sc in each st around. (12 sc) At the end of the Round 11, change color to **MC.** Fasten off **Color A.**

Round 12: Working in **back loops** only, sc in each st around. (12 sc)

 - Start stuffing Leg firmly, adding more as you go.

Rounds 13-30: (*18 rounds*) Sc in each st around. (12 sc)

Last Row: Sc in each sc across to edge of Leg (*about 2-3 sc*). Fasten off and weave in ends.

Second Leg

Rounds 1-30: Repeat Rounds 1-30 of First Leg.

Last Row: Sc in each sc across to edge of Leg (*about 2-3 sc*), (*image 1*) changing to **Color A** in last st. Fasten off **MC.** Continue with Body.

Body

Round 1: (*Joining Legs*) With **Color A**, ch 4; working on First Leg, starting at inner leg (*both feet parallel*), sc in each of next 12 sts; working in starting ch-4, sc in each of next 4 ch; working on Second Leg, sc in each of next 12 sts; working on other side of starting chain, sc in each of next 4 ch. Mark last st. Move marker at the end of each round. (32 sc) (*image 2*)

Rounds 2-7: (*6 rounds*) Sc in each st around. (32 sc)

Round 8: Sc in each of next 24 sts, change to **Color B**. Move marker to last st worked. Move marker each round.

  - Start stuffing the Body firmly, adding more as you go.

Round 9: Working in **back loops** only, sc in each st around. (32 sc) *(image 3)*

Rounds 10-11: (*2 rounds*) Sc in each st around. (32 sc)

Round 12: [Sc in each of next 6 sts, dec] 4 times. (28 sc)

Round 13: Sc in each st around. (28 sc)

Round 14: Working in **back loops** only, sc in each st around. (28 sc)

Round 15: [Sc in each of next 5 sts, dec] 4 times. (24 sc)

Round 16: Sc in each st around. (24 sc)

Round 17: [Sc in each of next 4 sts, dec] 4 times. (20 sc)

Round 18: Sc in each st around. (20 sc)

  - Add more stuffing to Body.

Round 19: [Sc in each of next 3 sts, dec] 4 times. (16 sc)

Round 20: Sc in each st around. (16 sc)

Round 21: [Sc in each of next 2 sts, dec] 4 times. (12 sc)

Round 22: Sc in each st around, changing to color **MC** in last st. (12 sc) *(image 4)*

Round 23: With **MC**, sc in each st around. (12 sc)

Round 24: Sc in each st around. (12 sc) Do not fasten off. Continue with Head. Finish stuffing the Body.

Head

Round 1: Inc in each st around. (24 sc)

Round 2: [Sc in each of next 3 sts, inc in next st] 6 times. (30 sc)

Round 3: Sc in each of next 2 sts, inc in next st, [sc in each of next 4 sts, inc in next st] 5 times, sc in each next 2 sts. (36 sc)

Round 4: [Sc in each of next 5 sts, inc in next st] 6 times. (42 sc)

Round 5: Sc in each of next 3 sts, inc in next st, [sc in each of next 6 sts, inc in next st] 5 times, sc in each next 3 sts. (48 sc) *(image 5)*

Round 6: [Sc in each of next 7 sts, inc in next st] 6 times. (54 sc)

Optional: For more neck stability, fold and insert the chenille wire down the center of the opening. *(image 6)*

Rounds 7-18: (*12 rounds*) Sc in each st around. (54 sc)

Round 19: [Sc in each of next 7 sts, dec] 6 times. (48 sc)

Round 20: Sc in each st around. (48 sc)

Start stuffing Head firmly, adding more as you go.

Round 21: [Sc in each of next 6 sts, dec] 6 times. (42 sc)

Round 22: [Sc in each of next 5 sts, dec] 6 times. (36 sc)

Round 23: [Sc in each of next 4 sts, dec] 6 times. (30 sc)

Round 24: [Sc in each of next 3 sts, dec] 6 times. (24 sc)

Round 25: [Sc in each of next 2 sts, dec] 6 times. (18 sc)

Round 26: [Sc in next st, dec] 6 times. (12 sc)

  - Finish stuffing the Head.

Round 27: [Dec] 6 times. (6 sc) Fasten off, leaving a long tail.

Using the tail and yarn needle, close the opening, and weave in the end. *(image 7)*

Dress

Round 1: Holding the Body upside down, working in the unused front loops on Round 13, attach **Color B** to the last st worked, ch 2 *(counts as first hdc)*, hdc in same st, [2 hdc in next st] around; join with sl st to first hdc (*2nd ch of ch-2*). (56 hdc) *(image 8)*

Rounds 2-9: (*8 rounds*) Ch 2, [hdc in next st] around; join as before. (56 hdc)

At the end of Round 9, fasten off and weave in ends.

ARM (Make 2)

Note: *Only the Hand is stuffed – not the whole Arm.*

Round 1: With **MC**, make a magic ring, 6 sc in ring. (6 sc) Tug tail to close. Do not join. Mark last st. Move marker at the end of each round.

Round 2: [Sc in next st, inc in next st] 3 times. (9 sc)

Rounds 3-5: (*3 rounds*) Sc in each st around. (9 sc)

Round 6: Sc in each of next 3 sts, dec, sc in each of next 2 sts, dec. (7 sc)

Stuff the Hand lightly.

Rounds 7-19: (*13 rounds*) Sc in each st around. (7 sc)

At the end of the Round 19, change to **Color B.** Fasten off **MC.**

Rounds 20-24: (*4 rounds*) Sc in each st around. (7 sc)

- Flatten the last round.

Last Row: Working through both thicknesses, sc in each of next 3 sc. Fasten off, leaving a long tail for sewing. *(image 9)*

Position the Arms on either side of the Body at Round 21. Using long tails and yarn needle, sew them in place and weave in ends. *(image 10)*

APRON

Row 1: With **Color C**, ch 35, starting in 2ⁿᵈ ch from hook, sc in each of next 20 ch. Leave remaining 14 ch unworked *(for Apron Tie)*. (20 sc)

Row 2: Ch 2, turn, 2 hdc in first st, hdc in next st, [2 hdc in next st, hdc in next st] across. (30 sc)

Rows 3-9: (*7 rows*) Ch 2, turn, hdc in each st across. (30 hdc) At the end of Row 9, fasten off and weave in ends.

Apron Bib

Row 1: With Apron upside down, working in unused lps of ch-sts, skip first 6 ch, attach **Color C** to next ch, ch 2, hdc in same st, hdc in each of next 7 sts. (8 hdc). Leave remaining 6 sts unworked.

Rows 2-3: (*2 rows*) Ch 2, turn, hdc in each st across. (8 hdc)

At the end of Row 3, do not fasten off. Continue with Bib Strap.

Bib Strap

With **Color C**, ch 18. Fasten off, leaving a long tail for sewing. *(image 11)*.

Position and pin the Apron to the front of the Doll. Sew the Apron Tie around the waist.

Wrap the Bib Strap around the Neck and sew to the other corner of the Bib. *(image 12)*

SUN HAT

Round 1: With **Color D**, make a magic ring, 6 sc in ring. (6 sc) Tug tail to close. Do not join. Mark last st. Move marker at the end of each round.

Round 2: Inc in each st around. (12 sc)

Round 3: [Sc in next st, inc in next st] 6 times. (18 sc)

Round 4: [Sc in each of next 2 sts, inc in next st] 6 times. (24 sc)

Round 5: [Sc in each of next 3 sts, inc in next st] 6 times. (30 sc)

Round 6: [Sc in each of next 4 sts, inc in next st] 6 times. (36 sc)

Round 7: [Sc in each of next 5 sts, inc in next st] 6 times. (42 sc)

Round 8: [Sc in each of next 6 sts, inc in next st] 6 times. (48 sc)

Round 9: [Sc in each of next 7 sts, inc in next st] 6 times. (54 sc)

Rounds 10-18: (*9 rounds*) Sc in each st around. (54 sc) At the end of the round 18, change to **Color C** in last st.

Round 19: With **Color C**, working in **back loops** only, sc in each st around. (54 sc)

Round 20: Sc in each st around, *(image 13)* changing to **Color D** in last st. (54 sc)

Round 21: With **Color D**, working in **back loops** only, [sc in next st, inc in next st] around. (81 sc) *(image 14)*

Rounds 22-23: Sc in each st around. (81 sc) At the end of Round 23, fasten off and weave in ends.

- Using **Color E** and yarn needle, embroider two lines around Rounds 19 & 20 using back stitches. *(image 15)*

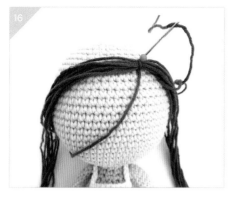

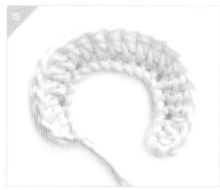

- Place the Hat on the Doll to determine the Hair position and continue with Hair Assembly.

HAIR ASSEMBLY

Cut 9 strands 18" (46 cm) long of **Color F**.

Holding the strands together, position them over the Head on top of the forehead at Round 20.

Using a separate strand of yarn, sew these long strands securely to Head.

Place the Hat on the Head to style the Hair – braiding the long strands on each side and securing the ends.

When Hair is complete, position the Hat on the Head and sew in place. *(image 16-17)*

COLLAR

Row 1: With **Color A**, ch 25, starting in the 2nd ch from hook, sc in next ch, hdc in next ch, 2 hdc in next ch, dc in each of next 3 ch, 2 dc in next ch, dc in each of next 10 ch, 2 dc in next ch, dc in each of next 3 ch, 2 hdc in next ch, hdc in next ch, sc in next ch. (28 sts) Fasten off, leaving a tail for sewing. *(image 18)*

SHOE (Make 2)

Round 1: With **Color E**, make a magic ring, 8 sc in ring. (8 sc) Tug tail to close. Do not join. Mark last st. Move marker at the end of each round.

Round 2: Inc in each st around. (16 sc)

Round 3: Sc in each of next 5 sts, inc in each of next 3 sts, sc in each of next 6 sts, inc in each of next 2 sts. (21 sc)

Round 4: Working in **back loops** only, sc in each st around. (21 sc)

Rounds 5-6: (*2 rounds*) Sc in each st around. (21 sc)

Round 7: Sc in each of next 5 sts, [dec] 4 times, sc in each of next 8 sts. (17 sc)

Round 8: Sc in each of next 3 sts, ch 7, skip next 8 sts, sc in each of next 5 sts, sl st in last st. (18 sc) Fasten off with Needle Join. *(image 19)*

FINISHING THE DOLL

With **Color A**, work a border on each Sock using the unused front loops of Round 11. You can embroider by whipstitching through each loop. *(image 20)* Or for a larger border, work either 12 slip stitches or 12 single crochet stitches around, ending with a Needle Join.

With the Floss, embroider the Eyes using vertical straight stitches on Round 9 of Head, with 11 stitches between them. *(image 21)*

Position the Collar around the Neck and sew in place. Place Shoes on Feet.

ACCESSORIES

BOHO BAG

Back Part

Round 1: With **Color G**, make a magic ring, 6 sc in ring. (6 sc) Tug tail to close. Do not join. Mark last st. Move marker at the end of each round.

Round 2: Inc in each st around. (12 sc)

Round 3: [Sc in next st, inc in next st) 6 times. (18 sc)

Round 4: [Sc in each of next 2 sts, inc in next st] 6 times. (24 sc)

Round 5: [Sc in each of next 3 sts, inc in next st] 6 times. (30 sc)

Round 6: [Sc in each of next 4 sts, inc in next st] 6 times. (36 sc)

Round 7: [Sc in each of next 5 sts, inc in next st] 6 times. (42 sc)

Last Row: Sl st in next st, ch 1, turn, working in **back loops** only, hdc in each of next 30 sts. Leave remaining sts unworked. (30 hdc) Fasten off. *(image 22)*

Front Part

Round 1: With **Color B**, ch 4; join with sl st to first ch to form a ring; ch 3 *(counts as first dc, now and throughout)*, 9 dc in ring; join with sl st to first dc *(3rd ch of ch-3)* (10 dc) Change color to **Color C**.

Round 2: With **Color C**, ch 3, *(image 23)* working in spaces between the stitches on Round 1, dc in next sp, [2 dc in next sp] around; join as before. (20 dc) Change color to **Color G**.

Round 3: With **Color G**, ch 2 *(counts as first hdc)*, working in spaces between the stitches on Round 2, 2 hdc in first sp, skip next sp, [3 hdc in next sp, skip next sp] around; join with sl st to first hdc *(2nd ch of ch-2)*. (30 hdc)

Round 4: [Sc in each of next 4 sts, inc in next st] 6 times. (36 sc) Fasten off, leaving a long tail for sewing. *(image 24)*

Bag Handle

With **Color G**, leaving a tail, ch 55. Fasten off, leaving a tail for sewing.

- Using the Handle tails, sew the ends of the Handle to the top of the Bag.

- Using the Front Part tail and yarn needle, sew the Front Part to the Back Part.

- Place Bag over Doll's shoulder.

BALLOON

Round 1: With **Color H**, make a magic ring, 6 sc in ring. (6 sc) Tug tail to close. Do not join. Mark last st. Move marker at the end of each round.

Round 2: Inc in each st around. (12 sc)

Round 3: [Sc in next st, inc in next st) 6 times. (18 sc)

Round 4: Sc in each st around. (18 sc)

Round 5: [Sc in each of next 2 sts, inc in next st] 6 times. (24 sc)

Rounds 6-10: *(5 rounds)* Sc in each st around. (24 sc)
- Start stuffing Balloon firmly, adding more as you go.

Round 11: [Sc in each of next 2 sts, dec] 6 times. (18 sc)

Round 12: Sc in each st around. (18 sc)

Round 13: [Sc in next st, dec] 6 times. (12 sc)

Round 14: Sc in each st around. (12 sc)

Round 15: [Dec] 6 times. (6 sc)

- Finish stuffing the Balloon.

Round 16: 2 hdc in each st around. (12 hdc) Fasten off, leaving a tail.

Wind the tail tightly around Round 15, and secure. Use the remaining tail as Balloon's string, or you can use a separate strand of yarn or a lollipop stick. *(image 25)*.

LOLLIPOP

First Coil

Row 1: With **Color A**, ch 41; starting in 2nd ch from hook, sc in each ch across. (40 sc) Fasten off, leaving a tail for sewing.

Second Coil

Row 1: With **Color H**, ch 53; starting in 2nd ch from hook, sc in each ch across. (52 sc) Fasten off, leaving a tail for sewing.

- Place the First Coil on the Second Coil and roll up them up together to form a snail. *(image 26)*

- Using the tails, sew the Coils in shape.

- Slide a Toothpick up from the bottom. *(image 27)*

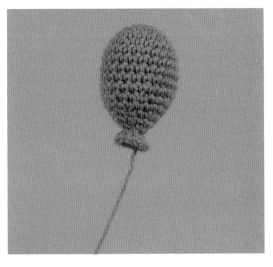

Matilda

designer
Sandra Muller
@luciennecompotine

Materials & Tools

HELLO Cotton Yarn

» **Main Color (MC):** Beige (157) - for Body
» **Color A:** White (154) - for Socks, Shorts & Collar
» **Color B:** Baby Pink (101) - for Dress
» **Color C:** Sea Green (136) - for Hat
» **Color D:** Gray (159) - for Jacket
» **Color E:** Dark Brown (127) - for Hair
» **Color F:** Mocha (125) - for Shoes & School Bag
» **Color G:** Light Brown (128) - for Hat Band & Teddy Bear

Other

» Stitch Markers
» Yarn Needle
» Stuffing
» Straight Pins
» DMC Embroidery Floss - Black (for Eyes)
» Embroidery Needle
» **Optional:** 12″ long Chenille Wire (Pipe Cleaner) – for neck stability

Hook Size

» 2.5 mm hook

Safety Note: This toy is not suitable for a child or infant when Wire is used in the Doll, as it could be a poking hazard. For a safer alternative, do not insert the Chenille Wire when making the Doll.

Finished Size

About 11″ (27 cm) tall

Skill Level

Intermediate

DOLL

BODY & HEAD

First Leg

Round 1: With **Color A**, make a magic ring, 7 sc in ring. (7 sc) Tug tail to close. Do not join. Mark last st. Move marker at the end of each round.

Round 2: Inc in each st around. (14 sc)

Rounds 3-4: (*2 rounds*) Sc in each st around. (14 sc)

Round 5: Sc in each of next 5 sts, [dec] twice, sc in each of next 5 sts. (12 sc)

Rounds 6-11: (*6 rounds*) Sc in each st around. (12 sc)

At the end of the Round 11, change color to **MC**.

Round 12: Working in **back loops** only, sc in each st around. (12 sc)

- Start stuffing Leg firmly, adding more as you go.

Rounds 13-23: (*11 rounds*) Sc in each st around. (12 sc)

At the end of the Round 23, change to **Color A**.

Fasten off MC.

Round 24: Sc in each st around. (12 sc)

Round 25: Working in **back loops** only, [sc in next st, inc in next st] around. (18 sc)

Rounds 26-27: (*2 rounds*) Sc in each st around. (18 sc)

Round 28: [Sc in each of next 4 sts, dec] 3 times. (15 sc)

Round 29: Sc in each st around. (15 sc)

Round 30: [Sc in each of next 3 sts, dec] 3 times. (12 sc)

Last Row: Sc in each sc across to edge of Leg (*about 2-3 sc*). Fasten off and weave in ends.

Second Leg

Rounds 1-30: Repeat Rounds 1-30 of First Leg.

Last Row: Sc in each sc across to edge of Leg (*about 2-3 sc*). (*image 1*) Do not fasten off. Continue with Body.

Body

Round 1: (*Joining Legs*) Ch 4; working on First Leg, starting at inner leg (*both feet parallel*), sc in each of next 12 sts; working in starting ch-4, sc in each of next 4 ch; working on Second Leg, sc in each of next 12 sts; working on other side of starting chain, sc in each of next 4 ch. Mark last st. Move marker at the end of each round. (32 sc) (*image 2*)

Rounds 2-7: (*6 rounds*) Sc in each st around. (32 sc)

Round 8: Sc in each of next 24 sts, change to **Color B**. Move marker to last st worked. Move marker each round.

- Start stuffing the Body firmly, adding more as you go.

Round 9: Working in **back loops** only, sc in each st around, changing to **Color B** in last st. (32 sc)

Rounds 10-11: (*2 rounds*) Sc in each st around. (32 sc)

Round 12: [Sc in each of next 6 sts, dec] 4 times. (28 sc)

Rounds 13-14: (*2 rounds*) Sc in each st around. (28 sc)

Round 15: [Sc in each of next 5 sts, dec] 4 times. (24 sc)

Round 16: Sc in each st around. (24 sc)

Round 17: [Sc in each of next 4 sts, dec] 4 times. (20 sc)

Round 18: Sc in each st around. (20 sc)

- Add more stuffing to Body.

Round 19: [Sc in each of next 3 sts, dec] 4 times. (16 sc)

Round 20: Sc in each st around. (16 sc)

Round 21: [Sc in each of next 2 sts, dec] 4 times. (12 sc)

Round 22: Sc in each st around, changing to color **MC** in last st. (12 sc)

Round 23: With **MC**, working in **back loops** only, sc in each st around. (12 sc) (*image 3*)

Round 24: Sc in each st around. (12 sc) Remove hook from loop (*to continue with Head later*). Do not fasten off. Continue with the Dress.

Dress

Round 1: Holding the Body upside down, working in the unused front loops on Round 22, attach **Color B** to the last st worked (*image 4*), ch 1, sc in each st around. (12 sc)

Round 2: [Sc in each of next 2 sts, inc in next st] 4 times. (16 sc)

Round 3: [Sc in each of next 3 sts, inc in next st] 4 times. (20 sc)

Round 4: [Sc in each of next 4 sts, inc in next st] 4 times. (24 sc)

Round 5: [Sc in each of next 5 sts, inc in next st] 4 times. (28 sc)

Rounds 6-7: (*2 rounds*) Sc in each st around. (28 sc)

Round 8: [Sc in each of next 6 sts, inc in next st] 4 times. (32 sc)

Rounds 9-11: (*3 rounds*) Sc in each st around. (32 sc)

Round 12: [Sc in each of next 7 sts, inc in next st] 4 times. (36 sc)

Round 13: Sc in each st around. (36 sc)

Round 14: [Sc in each of next 5 sts, inc in next st] 6 times. (42 sc)

Rounds 15-16: (*2 rounds*) Sc in each st around. (42 sc)

Round 17: [Sc in each of next 6 sts, inc in next st] 6 times. (48 sc)

Rounds 18-21: (*4 rounds*) Sc in each st around. (48 sc)

Round 22: [Sc in each of next 7 sts, inc in next st] 6 times. (54 sc)

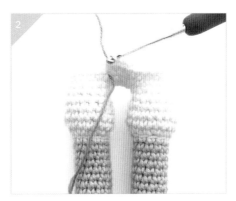

Round 23: Sc in each st around. (54 sc) Fasten off with Needle Join and weave in ends. *(image 5)*

Head

Insert hook in MC loop on Body.

Round 1: Inc in each st around. (24 sc)

Round 2: [Sc in each of next 3 sts, inc in next st] 6 times. (30 sc)

Round 3: Sc in each of next 2 sts, inc in next st, [sc in each of next 4 sts, inc in next st] 5 times, sc in each next 2 sts. (36 sc)

Round 4: [Sc in each of next 5 sts, inc in next st] 6 times. (42 sc)

Round 5: Sc in each of next 3 sts, inc in next st, [sc in each of next 6 sts, inc in next st] 5 times, sc in each next 3 sts. (48 sc) *(image 6)*

Round 6: [Sc in each of next 7 sts, inc in next st] 6 times. (54 sc)

- **Optional:** For more neck stability, fold and insert the

chenille wire down the center of the opening. *(image 7)*

Rounds 7-18: (*12 rounds*) Sc in each st around. (54 sc)

Round 19: [Sc in each of next 7 sts, dec] 6 times. (48 sc)

Round 20: Sc in each st around. (48 sc)

- Start stuffing Head firmly, adding more as you go.

Round 21: [Sc in each of next 6 sts, dec] 6 times. (42 sc)

Round 22: [Sc in each of next 5 sts, dec] 6 times. (36 sc)

Round 23: [Sc in each of next 4 sts, dec] 6 times. (30 sc)

Round 24: [Sc in each of next 3 sts, dec] 6 times. (24 sc)

Round 25: [Sc in each of next 2 sts, dec] 6 times. (18 sc)

Round 26: [Sc in next st, dec] 6 times. (12 sc)

- Finish stuffing the Head.

Round 27: [Dec] 6 times. (6 sc) Fasten off, leaving a long tail.

- Using the tail and yarn needle, close the opening, and weave in the end. *(image 8)*

ARM (Make 2)

Note: *Only the Hand is stuffed – not the whole Arm.*

Round 1: With **MC**, make a magic ring, 6 sc in ring. (6 sc) Tug tail to close. Do not join. Mark last st. Move marker at the end of each round.

Round 2: [Sc in next st, inc in next st] 3 times. (9 sc)

Rounds 3-5: (*3 rounds*) Sc in each st around. (9 sc)

Round 6: Sc in each of next 3 sts, dec, sc in each of next 2 sts, dec. (7 sc)

  - Stuff the Hand lightly.

Rounds 7-19: (*13 rounds*) Sc in each st around. (7 sc) At the end of the Round 19, change to **Color B.** Fasten off **MC**.

Rounds 20-24: (*4 rounds*) Sc in each st around. (7 sc)

  - Flatten the last round.

Last Row: Working through both thicknesses, sc in each of next 3 sc. Fasten off, leaving a long tail for sewing. *(image 9)*

- Position the Arms on either side of the Body at Round 21. Using long tails and yarn needle, sew them in place and weave in ends. *(image 10)*

COLLAR

Row 1: With **Color A**, ch 25, starting in the 2nd ch from hook, sc in next ch, hdc in next ch, 2 hdc in next ch, dc in each of next 3 ch, 2 dc in next ch, dc in each of next 10 ch, 2 dc in next ch, dc in each of next 3 ch, 2 hdc in next ch, hdc in next ch, sc in next ch. (28 sts) Fasten off, leaving a tail for sewing. *(image 11)*

HAT

Round 1: With **Color C**, make a magic ring, 6 sc in ring. (6 sc) Tug tail to close. Do not join. Mark last st. Move marker at the end of each round.

Round 2: Inc in each st around. (12 sc)

Round 3: [Sc in next st, inc in next st] 6 times. (18 sc)

Round 4: [Sc in each of next 2 sts, inc in next st] 6 times. (24 sc)

Round 5: [Sc in each of next 3 sts, inc in next st] 6 times. (30 sc)

Round 6: [Sc in each of next 4 sts, inc in next st] 6 times. (36 sc)

Round 7: [Sc in each of next 5 sts, inc in next st] 6 times. (42 sc)

Round 8: [Sc in each of next 6 sts, inc in next st] 6 times. (48 sc)

Round 9: [Sc in each of next 7 sts, inc in next st] 6 times. (54 sc)

Rounds 10-18: (*9 rounds*) Sc in each st around. (54 sc)

At the end of the round 18, change to **Color G** in last st.

Rounds 19-20: (*2 rounds*) Sc in each st around. (54 sc)

At the end of the Round 20, change to **Color C** in last st. Fasten off Color G.

Round 21: [Sc in each of next 2 sts, inc in next st] around. (72 sc)

Rounds 22-23: Sc in each st around. (72 sc)

At the end of Round 23, fasten off with Needle Join and weave in ends. *(image 12)*

- Place the Hat on the Doll to determine the Hair position and continue with Hair Assembly.

HAIR ASSEMBLY

Cut 9 strands 18" (46 cm) long of **Color E.**

Holding the strands together, position them over the Head on top of the forehead at Round 20.

Using a separate double strand of yarn, sew these long strands securely to Head. Trim the yarn tails to look like bangs.

Place the Hat on the Head to style the Hair – braiding the long strands on each side and securing the ends.

When Hair is complete, position the Hat on the Head and sew in place. *(image 13-14)*

COAT

Row 1: (Right Side) With **Color D**, ch 26, starting in 2nd ch from hook, sc in each ch across. (25 sc)

Row 2: Ch 1, turn, inc in first st, sc in each of next 11 st, inc in next st, sc in each of next 11 st, inc in last st. (28 sc)

Row 3: Ch 1, turn, sc in each of first 4 sts, ch 6, skip next 6 sts *(armhole)*, sc in each of next 8 sts, ch 6, skip next 6 sts *(armhole)*, sc in each of next 4 sts. (16 sc & 2 ch-6 lps)

Row 4: Ch 1, turn, sc in each of first 3 sts, inc in next st, *working in ch-6 lp, sc in each of next 6 ch, inc in next st*, sc in each of next 6 sts, inc in next st; repeat from * to * once, sc in each of next 3 sts. (32 sc)

Row 5: Ch 1, turn, sc in each st across. (32 sc) *(image 15)*

Row 6: Ch 1, turn, inc in first st, sc in each of next 9 sts, inc in next st, sc in each of next 10 sts, inc in next st, sc in each of next 9 sts, inc in last st. (36 sc)

Rows 7-10: (*4 rows*) Ch 1, turn, sc in each st across. (36 sc)

Row 11: Ch 1, turn, inc in first st, sc in each of next 10 sts, inc in next st, sc in each of next 12 sts, inc in next st, sc in each of next 10 sts, inc in last st. (40 sc)

Rows 12-17: (*6 rows*) Ch 1, turn, sc in each st across. (40 sc)

Row 18: Ch 1, turn, inc in first st, sc in each of next 38 sts, inc in last st. (42 sc)

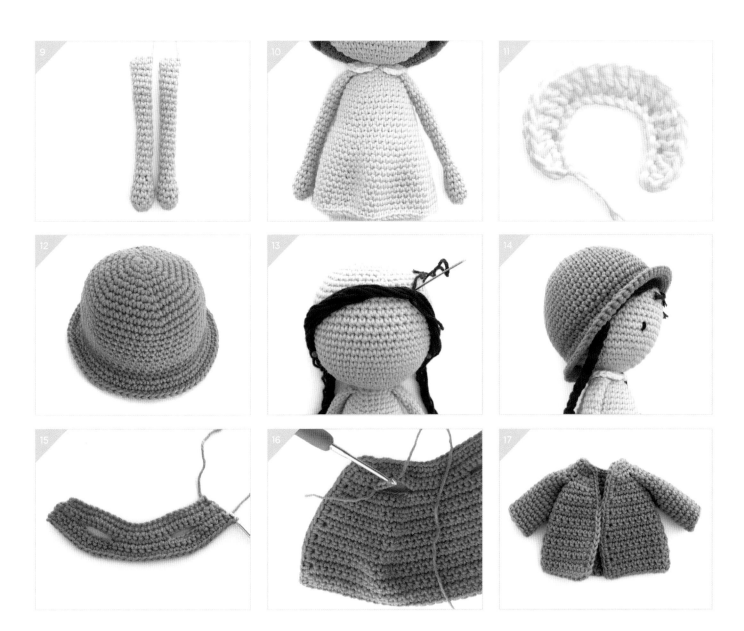

Row 19: Ch 1, turn, sc in each st across. (42 sc)

Edging Round: Ch 1, turn, sc in each st across; working in side of rows, sc in each row across; working on other side of starting chain, sc in each ch across; working in sides of rows, sc in each row across. Fasten off with Needle Join and weave in ends.

Coat Sleeves

Round 1: With right side facing, working around armholes, attach **Color D** with sl st to side of Row 3; working in skipped sts on Row 2, sc in each of next 6 sts *(image 16)*, sc in side of Row 3, working on other side ch-6, sc in each of next 6 ch, sc in side of Row 3 *(same st as sl st)*. Do not join. Mark last st. Move marker at the end of each round.

Rounds 2-13: Sc in each sc around. (14 sc)

Last Row: Sc in each st across to back of Coat. Fasten off with Needle Join and weave in ends.

Repeat for other Sleeve. *(image 17)*

SHOE (Make 2)

Round 1: With **Color F**, make a magic ring, 8 sc in ring. (8 sc) Tug tail to close. Do not join. Mark last st. Move marker at the end of each

Round 2: Inc in each st around. (16 sc)

Round 3: Sc in each of next 5 sts, inc in each of next 3 sts, sc in each of next 6 sts, inc in each of next 2 sts. (21 sc)

Round 4: Working in **back loops** only, sc in each st around. (21 sc)

Rounds 5-6: *(2 rounds)* Sc in each st around. (21 sc)

Round 7: Sc in each of next 5 sts, [dec] 4 times, sc in each of next 8 sts. (17 sc)

Round 8: Sc in each of next 3 sts, ch 7, skip next 8 sts, sc in each of next 5 sts, sl st in last st. (18 sc) Fasten off with Needle Join. *(image 18)*

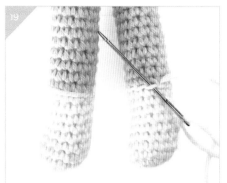

FINISHING THE DOLL

- With **Color A**, work a border on each Sock using the unused front loops of Round 11. You can embroider by whipstitching through each loop. *(image 19)* Or for a larger border, work either 12 slip stitches or 12 single crochet stitches around, ending with a Needle Join.

- With the Floss, embroider the Eyes using vertical straight stitches on Round 9 of Head, with 11 stitches between them. *(image 20)*

- Position the Collar around the Neck and sew in place.

- Place Shoes on Feet. *(image 21)*

ACCESSORIES

SCHOOL BAG

Bag Base

Row 1: With **Color F**, ch 15, starting in 2nd ch from hook, sc in each ch across. (14 sc)

Row 2: Ch 1, turn, sc in each st across.

Bag Sides

Round 1: Rotate base, working in sides of rows, sc in each of next 2 rows; working on other side of starting chain, sc in each ch across; working in sides of rows, sc in each of next 2 rows; working in Row 2, sc in each st across. (32 sc) Do not join. Mark last st. Move marker at the end of each round.

Rounds 2-10: Sc in each sc around. (32 sc)

Last Row: Sc in each of next 17 sc *(to reach edge of Bag)* Do not fasten off. Continue with Flap.

Bag Flap

Row 1: Ch 1, turn, sc in first st, sc in each of next 13 sts. (14 sc) Leave remaining sts unworked.

Rows 2-9: Ch 1, turn, sc in each st across. (14 sc)
At the end of Row 9, fasten off and weave in ends.

Bag Strap

Row 1: With **Color F**, ch 54, starting in 2nd ch from hook, sl st in each ch across. Fasten off, leaving a long tail for sewing.

- Position and sew the Strap to either side of the Bag. *(image 22)*

TEDDY BEAR

Round 1: Starting at Head, with **Color G**, make a magic ring, 6 sc in ring. (6 sc) Tug tail to close. Do not join. Mark last st. Move marker at the end of each round.

Round 2: Inc in each st around. (12 sc)

Round 3: [Sc in next st, inc in next st] 6 times. (18 sc)

Round 4: [Sc in each of next 2 sts, inc in next st] 6 times. (24 sc)

Rounds 5-8: *(4 rounds)* Sc in each st around. (24 sc)

- Stuff Head firmly, adding more as you go.

Round 9: [Sc in each of next 2 sts, dec] 6 times. (18 sc)

Round 10: [Sc in next st, dec] 6 times. (12 sc)

Round 11: [Dec] 6 times. (6 sc)

Round 12: Sc in each sc around. (6 sc)

- Finish stuffing the Head.

Round 13: Inc in each st around. (12 sc)

Round 14: Sc in each sc around. (12 sc)

Round 15: [Sc in each of next 2 sts, inc in next st] 4 times. (16 sc)

Rounds 16-19: *(4 rounds)* Sc in each sc around. (16 sc)

Stuff Body.

First Leg

Round 1: Sc in next st & 9th st together *(skipping 8 sts)*, sc in each of next 6 sts. (7 sc)

Rounds 2-4: Sc in each st around. (7 sc)

- Finish stuffing Leg.

Round 5: [Dec] 3 times, sl st in last st. Fasten off, leaving a long tail.

- Using the long tail and yarn needle, close the opening, and weave in ends.

Second Leg

Round 1: Working in the 8 skipped sts on Rnd 19, join **Color G** with sl st to first skipped st, sc in same st & 8th st together, sc in each of next 6 sts. (7 sc)

Rounds 2-4: Sc in each st around. (7 sc)

- Finish stuffing Leg.

Round 5: [Dec] 3 times, sl st in last st. Fasten off, leaving a long tail.

- Using the long tail and yarn needle, close the opening, and weave in ends.

- Using the Black Floss, embroider the Teddy Eyes on Round 7, with 6 stitches between them.

- Embroider a Nose between the Eyes.

Teddy Arm (Make 2)

Round 1: With **Color G**, make a magic ring, 5 sc in ring. (5 sc) Tug tail to close. Do not join. Mark last st. Move marker at the end of each round.

Rounds 2-6: Sc in each sc around. (5 sc) At the end of Round 6, fasten off, leaving a long tail for sewing.

- Using the tail, close the opening.

- Position the Arms on either side of Teddy Body and sew in place.

Teddy Ear (Make 2)

Round 1: With **Color G**, make a magic ring, 6 sc in ring. (6 sc) Tug tail to close. Fasten off, leaving a long tail for sewing.

- Position the Ears on either side of Teddy Head and using the tails, sew in place. *(image 23)*

emily The Gardener

designer

Damla Savaş
@yesiltosba

Materials & Tools

HELLO Cotton Yarn

- » **Main Color (MC):** Beige (157) - for Body
- » **Color A:** Yellow (123) - for Boots & Watering Can
- » **Color B:** Cherry Red (113) - for Sweater & Cherries
- » **Color C:** Off-White (155) - for Sweater
- » **Color D:** Dark Beige (158) - for Hat
- » **Color E:** Brown (126) - for Hat Band
- » **Color F:** Gray Blue (149) - for Overalls
- » **Color G:** Sage (137) - for Cherry Leaves

Hook Size

- » 2.5 mm hook
- » 3.0 mm hook – for Hair, Clothes & Accessories

Other

- » Stitch Markers
- » Yarn Needle
- » Stuffing
- » Mohair yarn (Medium Weight) – for Hair
- » Safety Eyes - Black Round (9 mm) x 2
- » ¼" (0.8 cm) Wooden Beads x 2 - for Overalls
- » Embroidery Needle
- » Cosmetic Blusher

Finished Size

About 9½" (24 cm) tall

Skill Level

Advanced

79

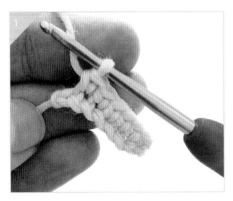

DOLL

BOOT (Make 2)

Round 1: With **Color A** and smaller hook, ch 8; starting in 2ⁿᵈ ch from hook, sc in each of next 6 ch, *(image 1)* 3 sc in last ch, working on other side of starting chain, sc in each of next 5 ch, 3 sc in last ch. (17 sc) Do not join. Mark last st. Move marker at the end of each round.

Round 2: 2 dc in next st, hdc in next st, sc in each of next 5 sts, 2 hdc in each of next 2 sts, sc in each of next 3 sts, hdc in each of next 2 sts, 2 dc in next st, hdc in each of next 2 sts. (21 sts) *(image 2)*

Round 3: Working in **back loops** only, inc in next st, sc in each of next 7 sts, inc in each of next 2 sts, sc in each of next 7 sts, [2 hdc in next st, hdc in next st] 2 times. (26 sts)

Round 4: Hdc in each of next 2 sts, sc in each of next 16 sts, [dec] 4 times. (22 sts)

Round 5: [Dec] 3 times, sc in each of next 12 sts, [dec] 2 times. (17 sc)

Round 6: [Dec] 2 times, sc in each of next 11 sts, dec. (14 sc)

Round 7: Dec, sc in each of next 10 sts, dec. (12 sc) *(image 3)*

Round 8: Sc in each st around. (12 sc)

Round 9: [Sc in each of next 3 sts, inc in next st] 3 times. (15 sc)

Round 10: Working in **front loops** only, [sc in each of next 4 sts, inc in next st] 3 times. (18 sc)

Round 11: Sc in each st around. (18 sc)

Round 12: Sc in each of next 9 sts, inc in next st, sc in each of next 8 sts. (19 sc)

Last Row: Sc in each of next 4 sts, sl st in next st. Fasten off and weave in ends.

- Stuff the Boot.

First Leg

Round 1: Working in unused back loops on Round 9 of Boot, attach **MC**, sc in each st around. (15 sc) *(image 4-6)*

Rounds 2-14: *(13 rounds)* Sc in each sc around. (15 sc) At the end of Round 14, fasten off and weave in ends.

Second Leg

Rounds 1-14: Repeat Rounds 1-14 of First Leg.
At the end of Round 14, do not fasten off. Continue with Body.

- Stuff the Legs.

BODY

Round 1: *(Joining Legs)* Ch 5, working on First Leg, sc in any st at inner leg *(making sure the feet face the same way)*, sc in each of next 14 sts, working in ch-5, sc in each of next 5 ch, working on Second Leg, sc in each of next 15 sts, working on other side of ch-5, sc in each of next 5 ch, changing to **Color B** in last st. (40 sc) Mark last st made. Move marker at the end of each round.

Rounds 2-3: With **Color B**, sc in each st around. (40 sc) *(image 7)*

At end of Round 3, work 8 more sc to end at side edge of Doll, changing to **Color C** in last st. Drop **Color B** to inside. Mark last sc as new end of round. Move marker each round.

Note: *For Rounds 4-25, alternate **Color C** and **Color B** at the end of each round, dropping the unused color to the inside.*

Rounds 4-21: *(18 rounds)* Sc in each st around. (40 sc) *(image 8-9)*

- Start stuffing Body, adding more as you go.

Round 22: With **Color C**, [sc in each of next 3 sts, dec] 8 times. (32 sc)

Round 23: With **Color B**, [sc in each of next 2 sts, dec] 8 times. (24 sc)

Round 24: With **Color C**, [sc in each of next 4 sts, dec] 4 times. (20 sc)

Round 25: With **Color B**, [sc in each of next 8 sts, dec] 2 times, changing to **MC** in last st. (18 sc) Fasten off **Color B** & **Color C**.

Round 26: Working in **back loops** only, with **MC** sc in each st around. (18 sc)

Round 27: Sc in each st around. (18 sc)

Round 28: [Dec] 2 times, sc in each of next 14 sts. (16 sc)

Round 29: Dec, sc in each of next 14 sts. (15 sc) Fasten off.

HEAD

Round 1: With **MC** and smaller hook, make a magic ring, 5 sc in ring. (5 sc) Tug tail to tighten ring. Do not join. Mark last st. Move marker at the end of each round.

Round 2: [Inc in next st] 5 times. (10 sc)

Round 3: [Inc in next st] 10 times. (20 sc)

Round 4: [Sc in each of next 3 sts, inc in next st] 5 times. (25 sc)

Round 5: [Sc in each of next 4 sts, inc in next st] 5 times. (30 sc)

Round 6: [Sc in each of next 4 sts, inc in next st] 6 times. (36 sc)

Round 7: Sc in each st around. (36 sc)

Round 8: [Sc in each of next 8 sts, inc in next st] 4 times. (40 sc)

Round 9: Sc in each st around. (40 sc)

Round 10: [Sc in each of next 9 sts, inc in next st] 4 times. (44 sc)

Round 11: Sc in each st around. (44 sc)

Round 12: [Sc in each of next 10 sts, inc in next st] 4 times. (48 sc)

Round 13: [Sc in each of next 11 sts, inc in next st] 4 times. (52 sc)

Rounds 14-22: *(9 rounds)* Sc in each st around. (52 sc)

Round 23: [Sc in each of next 11 sts, dec] 4 times. (48 sc)

Round 24: [Sc in each of next 4 sts, dec] 8 times. (40 sc)

- Insert Safety Eyes between Rounds 18 & 19, with about 11-12 stitches between them.

- Stuff Head firmly.

Round 25: [Sc in each of next 3 sts, dec] 8 times. (32 sc)

Round 26: [Sc in each of next 2 sts, dec] 8 times. (24 sc)

Round 27: [Sc in next st, dec] 8 times. (16 sc) Fasten off, leaving a long tail for sewing.

FINISHING THE FACE

- With **MC**, embroider a Nose between the Eyes, in line with the bottom of the Eyes, using a few straight stitches - about 2 stitches wide. *(image 10)*

- With **Color E**, embroider an outline around each Eye, using about 4-5 backstitches. *(image 10)*

- Embroider the Eyebrows using **Color E** about 3-4 rounds above the Eyes – about 3 stitches wide.

- Split a strand of **Color E**, and using the finer yarn, embroider Freckles randomly under each Eye.

- Add some Blusher to the cheeks.

ARM (Make 2)

Note: *Do not stuff Arms.*

Round 1: With **MC** and smaller hook, make a magic ring, 7 sc in ring. (7 sc) Tug tail to tighten ring. Do not join. Mark last st. Move marker at the end of each round.

Round 2: [Inc in next st] 7 times. (14 sc)

Rounds 3-4: *(2 rounds)* Sc in each st around. (14 sc)

Round 5: [Dec] 2 times, sc in each of next 10 sts. (12 sc)

Round 6: Sc in each st around, changing to **Color B** in last st. (12 sc)

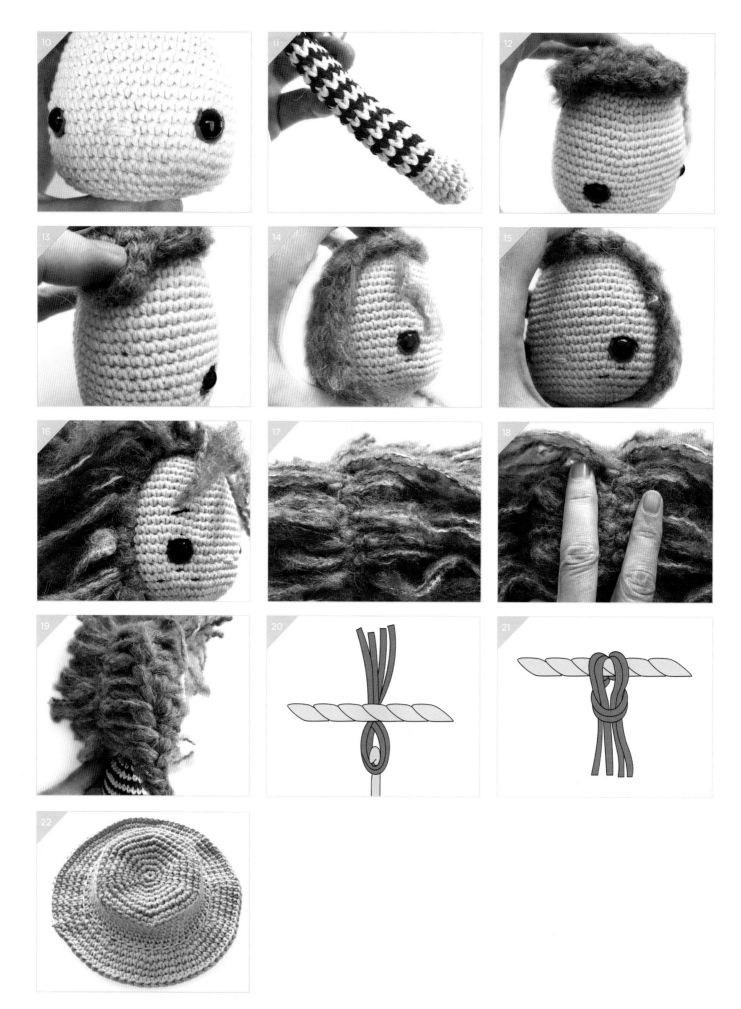

Note: For Rounds 7-27, alternate **Color B** and **Color C** at the end of each round, dropping the unused color to the inside.

Round 7: Working in **back loops** only, with B sc in each st around. (12 sc)

Rounds 8-27: *(21 rounds)* Sc in each st around. (12 sc)

At the end of Round 27, flatten the last round. Working through both thicknesses, sc in each of next 6 sc. Fasten off, leaving a long tail of **Color B** for sewing. *(image 11)*

ASSEMBLY OF DOLL

Head - Position the Head over the neck of the Body (adding more stuffing, if needed), with the last round of the Body inside the Head. Using the long tail, sew the Head firmly to Round 28 of the Body, matching stitches.

Arms - Position each Arm on either side of Body between Rounds 24 & 25. Using long tails, sew in place.

HAIR

Note: As there are so many different types and thicknesses of Mohair yarn, it is easier to first make a Hair Cap to fit the Head, and then attach the Hair to the Cap. For this reason, you might need to adjust the number of stitches, as well as the number of rounds and/or rows in the Hair Cap pattern so that the fits the doll's head. For example, with thicker yarn you might only need 8-9 rows. Using finer yarn you might need 11-12 rows. As you are making the Cap, keep fitting it on the Head.

Hair Cap

Round 1: With Mohair yarn and larger hook, make a magic ring, 8 sc in ring. (8 sc) Tug tail to tighten ring. Do not join. Mark last st. Move marker at the end of each round.

Round 2: [Inc in next st] 8 times. (16 sc)

Round 3: [Sc in next st, inc in next st] 8 times. (24 sc) Work continues in Rows.

Row 4: Sc in each of next 14 sts. (14 sc) Leave remaining stitches unworked. (The remaining stitches should be as wide as the face.) *(image 12)*

Row 5: Ch 1, turn, [sc in each of next 6 sts, inc in next st] 2 times. (16 sc)

Row 6: Ch 1, turn, [sc in each of next 7 sts, inc in next st] 2 times. (18 sc) *(image 13)*

Row 7: Ch 1, turn, [sc in each of next 8 sts, inc in next st] 2 times. (20 sc)

Row 8: Ch 1, turn, [sc in each of next 9 sts, inc in next st] 2 times. (22 sc)

Row 9: Ch 1, turn, [sc in each of next 10 sts, inc in next st] 2 times. (24 sc)

Rows 10-12: Ch 1, turn, sc in each st across. (24 sc) At the end of Round 12, fasten off and weave in ends.

 - Position the Cap on Head and sew in place. *(image 14-15)*

Attaching the Hair

Note: Feel free to change the number and length of the Hair strands to create your Doll's hair.

Cut 40-50 strands of Mohair all the same length - about 6"-8" (15-20 cm) long.

Using the photos as a guide (or designing the hairstyle yourself), attach the strands on either side of the Hair Cap - down the center back, along the base, and around the face. *(image 16-19)*

To Attach

Fold each strand in half. Insert hook under stitch and place folded end on hook. Pull the strand halfway through to form a loop. Then thread the strand tails through the loop and tug the tails to tighten. *(image 20-21)*

HAT

Round 1: With **Color D** and larger hook, make a magic ring, 6 sc in ring. (6 sc) Tug tail to tighten ring. Do not join. Mark last st. Move marker at the end of each round.

Round 2: [Inc in next st] 6 times. (12 sc)

Round 3: [Sc in next st, inc in next st] 6 times. (18 sc)

Round 4: [Sc in each of next 2 sts, inc in next st] 6 times. (24 sc)

Round 5: [Sc in each of next 3 sts, inc in next st] 6 times. (30 sc)

Round 6: [Sc in each of next 4 sts, inc in next st] 6 times. (36 sc)

Round 7: [Sc in each of next 5 sts, inc in next st] 6 times. (42 sc)

Round 8: [Sc in each of next 6 sts, inc in next st] 6 times. (48 sc)

Round 9: Working in **back loops** only, sc in each st around. (48 sc)

Rounds 10-16: *(7 rounds)* Sc in each st around. (48 sc)

Round 17: Working in **back loops** only, [sc in next st, inc in next st] 24 times. (72 sc)

Round 18: [Sc in each of next 5 sts, inc in next st] 12 times. (84 sc)

Rounds 19-21: *(3 rounds)* Sc in each st around. (84 sc) At the end of Round 21, fasten off and weave in ends. *(image 22)*

Hat Band

Round 1: Working in unused front loops on Round 16, attach **Color E**, and work hdc in each st around. Fasten off and weave in ends. *(image 23-24)*

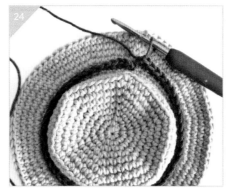

CHERRY (Make 2)

Round 1: With **Color B** and larger hook, make a magic ring, 6 sc in ring. (6 sc) Tug tail to tighten ring. Do not join.

Round 2: Sc in each st around. (6 sc)

Round 3: [Dec] 3 times (3 sc) Fasten off. *(image 25)*

Cherry Stem

With **Color G**, leaving a tail, ch 5, sl st in 2ⁿᵈ ch from hook, ch 3. Fasten off, leaving a tail for sewing.

Cherry Leaf

With **Color G**, ch 5; sc in 2ⁿᵈ ch from hook, hdc in next ch, dc in next ch, sl st in last ch. Fasten off, leaving a long tail for sewing.

Cherry Assembly

Using the tails, sew a Cherry to each end of the Cherry Stem. Sew the Leaf to a Cherry.

 - Position the Cherries on the Hat Band and sew in place. *(image 26)*

OVERALLS

Pants Leg (Make 2)

Round 1: With **Color F** and larger hook, ch 20; taking care not to twist ch, join with sl st to first ch to form a ring; ch 1, working in the top loops only of the ch-sts, sc in each ch around. (20 sc) Do not join. Mark last st. Move marker at the end of each round.

Rounds 2-9: (8 rounds) Sc in each st around. (20 sc) At the end of Round 9, for the First Leg, fasten off and

weave in ends. For the Second Leg continue with Pants. *(image 27-28)*

Pants

Round 1: *(Joining Legs)* Ch 1; working on First Leg, sc in each st around; working in ch-1, sc in next ch; working on Second Leg, sc in each st around; working on other side of ch-1, sc in next ch. (42 sc) Mark last st made. Move marker each round.

Rounds 2-7: *(6 rounds)* Sc in each st around. (42 sc)

Last Row: Sc in each of next 13 sts, sl st in next st. Fasten off and weave in ends.

Note: *The last slip stitch is at the side of the Pants.*

 - Mark the center 10 stitches at the front of the Pants.

Bib

Row 1: Attach Color F to first marked st, *(image 29)* ch 1, sc in each of next 10 sts. (10 sc)

Rows 2-6: *(5 rows)* Ch 1, turn, sc in each st across. (10 sc) At the end of Row 6, fasten off and weave in ends.

Strap (Make 2)

Row 1: With **Color F** and larger hook, starting with a long tail, ch 25; starting in 2ⁿᵈ ch from hook, sc in each of next 24 ch. (24 sc)

Row 2: Ch 1, turn, sc in each st across. (24 sc) Fasten off, leaving a tail for sewing. *(image 30)*

Pocket (Make 2)

Row 1: With **Color F** and larger hook, ch 6; starting in 2ⁿᵈ ch from hook, sc in each of next 5 ch. (5 sc)

Rows 2-4: Ch 1, turn, sc in each st across. (5 sc)

At the end of Row 4, fasten off, weaving in all ends. *(image 30)*

Assembly of Overalls

- Position the Pockets on the front of the Overalls. Using **Color C**, sew in place using straight stitches.
- Using the long tails, position and sew the one end of the Straps to the back of the Overalls, and the other end to the top of the Bib.
- Position and sew Buttons to Bib through Straps.
- Turn up the Pants Legs. *(image 31)*

WATERING CAN

Round 1: With **Color A** and larger hook, make a magic ring, 6 sc in ring. (6 sc) Tug tail to tighten ring. Do not join. Mark last st. Move marker at the end of each round.

Round 2: Inc in each st around. (12 sc)

Round 3: [Sc in next st, inc in next st] 6 times. (18 sc)

Round 4: Working in **back loops** only, sc in each st around. (18 sc)

Rounds 5-12: Sc in each st around. (18 sc) *(image 32)*

At the end of Round 12, ch 12 *(for Handle)*. Fasten off, leaving a long tail for sewing.

- Using the long tail, sew the end of the chain to the bottom of the Watering Can, to form a Handle.

Spout

Round 1: With **Color A** and larger hook, make a magic ring, 6 sc in ring. (6 sc) Tug tail to tighten ring. Do not join.

Mark last st. Move marker at the end of each round.

Round 2: [Sc in next st, inc in next st] 3 times. (9 sc)

Round 3: Working in **back loops** only, sc in each st around. (9 sc)

Round 4: [Sc in next st, dec] 3 times. (6 sc)

Round 5: Dec, sc in each of next 4 sts. (5 sc)

Rounds 6-7: Sc in each st around. (5 sc)

At the end of Round 7, fasten off leaving a long tail for sewing. *(image 33)*

- Using the long tail, sew the Spout to the bottom of the Watering Can (on the opposite side to the handle). *(image 34)*

Grandma & Grandpa

designer

Skaiste Kivci

@skaistekivci

Materials & Tools

HELLO Cotton Yarn

For Grandma

» **Main Color (MC):** Beige (157) - for Body

» **Color A:** Black (160) - for Shoes

» **Color B:** Brown (126) - for Hair

» **Color C:** Brick Red (117) - for Shawl

» **Color D:** Dark Green (135) - for Dress

For Grandpa

» **Main Color (MC):** Beige (157) - for Body

» **Color A:** Black (160) - for Shoes

» **Color B:** Brown (126) - for Hair

» **Color C:** Brick Red (117) - for Vest

» **Color E:** Dark Beige (158) - for Shirt

» **Color F:** Mustard (124) - for Pants

Hook Size

» 2.5 mm hook

Other

» Stitch Markers

» Yarn Needle

» Stuffing

» Straight Pins

» DMC Embroidery Floss - Black (for Eyes)

» Embroidery Needle

» Cosmetic Blusher

Finished Size

Grandma - About 11½" (29 cm) tall

Grandpa - About 11½" (28 cm) tall

Skill Level

Intermediate

SPECIAL STITCHES & TECHNIQUES

Puff Stitch (puff): [Yarn over hook, insert hook in specified stitch and pull up a loop (to height of an hdc-stitch)] 4 times, yarn over and draw through all 9 loops on the hook.

Double Crochet Decrease (dc2tog)

Yarn over hook, insert hook in stitch or space specified and pull up a loop *(3 loops on hook)*; yarn over and draw through 2 loops on hook *(2 loops remain)*; yarn over hook, insert hook in next the stitch or space and pull up a loop *(4 loops on hook)*; yarn over and draw through 2 loops on hook *(3 loops remain)*; yarn over and draw through all 3 loops on hook. Decrease made.

PATTERN NOTES

1. The body parts of the dolls are worked in spiral rounds.

2. The patterns for the Legs, Body, Arms, and Head are the same for both dolls.

3. Fill the body parts with stuffing as you go.

DOLL

BODY & HEAD

Body

For Grandma only:

Round 1: With **MC**, make a magic ring, 6 sc in ring. (6 sc) Do not join. Mark last st. Move marker at the end of each round.

For Grandpa only:

Round 1: With **Color E,** make a magic ring, 6 sc in ring. (6 sc) Do not join. Mark last st. Move marker at the end of each round.

For both Dolls:

Round 2: Inc in each sc around. (12 sc)

Round 3: [Sc in next st, inc in next st] 6 times. (18 sc)

Round 4: [Sc in each of next 2 sts, inc in next st] 6 times. (24 sc)

Round 5: [Sc in each of next 3 sts, inc in next st] 6 times. (30 sc)

Round 6: [Sc in each of next 4 sts, inc in next st] 6 times. (36 sc)

Round 7: [Sc in each of next 5 sts, inc in next st] 6 times. (42 sc)

For Grandma only:

Rounds 8-13: *(6 rounds)* Sc in each st around. (42 sc)

For Grandpa only:

Rounds 8-10: Sc in each st around. (42 sc)

Round 11: Working in **back loops** only, sc in each st around. (42 sc)

Rounds 12-13: *(2 rounds)* Sc in each st around. (42 sc)

For both Dolls:

Round 14: [Sc in each of next 5 sts, dec] 6 times. (36 sc)

Rounds 15-16: *(2 rounds)* Sc in each st around. (36 sc)

Round 17: [Sc in each of next 4 sts, dec] 6 times. (30 sc)

Rounds 18-19: *(2 rounds)* Sc in each st around. (30 sc)

Round 20: [Sc in each of next 3 sts, dec] 6 times. (24 sc)

Rounds 21-22: *(2 rounds)* Sc in each st around. (24 sc)

Round 23: [Sc in each of next 2 sts, dec] 6 times. (18 sc)

For Grandma only:

Round 24: Sc in each st around. (18 sc)

Round 25: Working in **back loops** only, [sc in next st, dec] 6 times. (12 sc) *(image 1)*

Note: *If it would be easier for you, work Grandma's Dress first before continuing with the Head.*

For Grandpa only:

Round 24: Sc in each st around, changing to **MC** in last st. (18 sc)

Round 25: With **MC**, working in **back loops** only, [sc in next st, dec] 6 times. (12 sc) *(image 2)*

For both Dolls:

Head

Round 26: Inc in each st around. (24 sc)

Round 27: Sc in each st around. (24 sc)

Round 28: [Sc in each of next 2 sts, inc in next st] 8 times. (32 sc)

Round 29: [Sc in each of next 3 sts, inc in next st] 8 times. (40 sc)

Round 30: [Sc in each of next 4 sts, inc in next st] 8 times. (48 sc)

Round 31: [Sc in each of next 5 sts, inc in next st] 8 times. (56 sc)

Round 32: [Sc in each of next 6 sts, inc in next st] 8 times. (64 sc)

Round 33: Sc in each of next 20 sts, [inc in next st, sc in

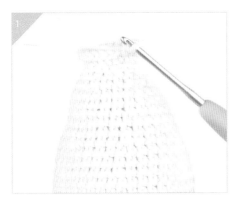

each of next 2 sts, inc in next st, sc in each of next 16 sc] 2 times, sc in each of next 4 sts. (68 sc)

Rounds 34-37: *(4 rounds)* Sc in each st around. (68 sc)

Round 38: Sc in each of next 20 sts, [dec, sc in each of next 2 sts, dec, sc in each of next 16 sc] 2 times, sc in each of next 4 sts. (64 sc)

Round 39: Sc in each of next 19 sts, [dec, sc in each of next 2 sts, dec, sc in each of next 14 sc] 2 times, sc in each of next 5 sts. (60 sc)

Round 40: [Sc in each of next 8 sts, dec] 6 times. (54 sc)

Rounds 41-47: *(7 rounds)* Sc in each st around. (54 sc)

Round 48: [Sc in each of next 7 sts, dec] 6 times. (48 sc)

Round 49: [Sc in each of next 6 sts, dec] 6 times. (42 sc)

Round 50: [Sc in each of next 5 sts, dec] 6 times. (36 sc)

Round 51: [Sc in each of next 4 sts, dec] 6 times. (30 sc)

Round 52: [Sc in each of next 3 sts, dec] 6 times. (24 sc)

Round 53: [Sc in each of next 2 sts, dec] 6 times. (18 sc)

Round 54: [Sc in next st, dec] 6 times. (12 sc)

Round 55: [Dec] 6 times. (6 sc) Fasten off, leaving a long tail.

- Using long tail and yarn needle, close the opening. *(image 3)*

LEG (Make 2)

Round 1: With **Color A**, ch 6; inc in 2nd ch from hook, sc in each of next 3 ch, 3 sc in last ch; working on other side of starting chain, sc in each of next 4 ch. (12 sc) Do not join. Mark last st made. Move marker at the end of each round.

Round 2: Inc in each each of next 2 sts, sc in each of next 3 sts, inc in each of next 3 sts, sc in each of next 3 sts, inc in last st. (18 sc)

Round 3: [Sc in next st, inc in next st] 2 times, sc in each of next 3 sts, [sc in next st, inc in next st] 3 times, sc in each of next 4 sts, inc in last st. (24 sc)

Round 4: Working in **back loops** only, sc in each st around. (24 sc)

Rounds 5-6: *(2 rounds)* Sc in each st around. (24 sc)

Round 7: Sc in each of next 9 sts, [dec, sc in next st] 3

times, sc in each of next 6 sts. (21 sc)

Round 8: Sc in each of next 9 sts, [dec] 3 times, sc in each of next 6 sts, changing to **MC** in last st. (18 sc)

Round 9: With **MC**, working in **back loops** only, sc in next st, dec, sc in each of next 4 sts, dec, sc in each of next 3 sts, dec, sc in each of next 4 sts. (15 sc) *(image 4)*

Rounds 10-29: *(20 rounds)* Sc in each st around. (15 sc)

At the end of Round 29, sc in each of next 3 sts, to end at front of Leg.

- Finish stuffing Leg.

Last Row: Flatten Leg, working through both thicknesses, sc in each of next 7 sts. (7 sc) Fasten off, leaving a long tail for sewing. *(image 5)*

- Position the Legs on either side of the Body at Round 8, and using long tails, sew in place. *(image 6-7)*

ARM (Make 2)

Round 1: With **MC**, make a magic ring, 6 sc in ring. (6 sc) Do not join. Mark last st. Move marker at the end of each round.

Round 2: [Sc in next st, inc in next st] 3 times. (9 sc)

Round 3: [Sc in each of next 2 sts, inc in next st] 3 times. (12 sc)

Rounds 4-5: *(2 rounds)* Sc in each st around. (12 sc)

Round 6: Sc in each of next 5 sts, **puff** in next st *(thumb)*, *(image 8-9)* sc in each of next 6 sts. (11 sc & 1 puff stitch)

For Grandma only:

Round 7: [Sc in each of next 2 sts, dec] 3 times, changing to **Color D** in last st. (9 sc)

- Stuff Hand firmly.

Round 8: With **Color D**, sc in each st around. (9 sc)

For Grandpa only:

Round 7: [Sc in each of next 2 sts, dec] 3 times, changing to **Color E** in last st. (9 sc)

- Stuff Hand firmly.

Round 8: With **Color E**, sc in each st around. (9 sc)

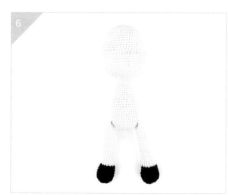

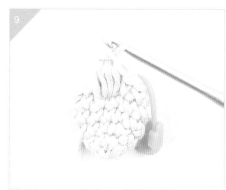

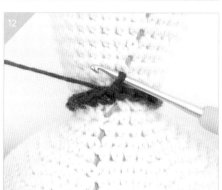

For both Dolls:

Round 9: [Sc in each of next 2 sts, inc in next st] 3 times. (12 sc)

Round 10: [Sc in each of next 3 sts, inc in next st] 3 times. (15 sc)

Rounds 11-14: *(4 rounds)* Sc in each st around. (15 sc)

Round 15: [Sc in each of next 3 sts, dec] 3 times. (12 sc)

Rounds 16-23: *(8 rounds)* Sc in each st around. (12 sc)
At the end of Round 23, sc in each of next 4 sts, to end at edge of Arm.

- Stuff only the bottom part of Arm.

Last Row: Flatten Arm, working through both thicknesses, sc in each of next 5 sts *(last st should be in line with the thumb)*. (5 sc) Fasten off, leaving a long tail for sewing. *(image 10)*

EAR (Make 2)

Round 1: With **MC**, make a magic ring, 6 sc in ring. (6 sc) Tug tail to tighten ring. Do not join. Fasten off, leaving long tail for sewing. *(image 11)*

GRANDMA

DRESS

Round 1: Holding the Body upside down, working in the unused front loops on Round 24, attach **Color D** to st at center back of Doll; sc in each st around; join with sl st to first sc. (18 sc) *(image 12)*

Round 2: Ch 2, working in **back loops** only, dc in same st as joining, 2 dc in next st, [dc in next st, 2 dc in next st] 8 times; join with sl st to first dc. (27 dc) *(image 13)*

Round 3: Ch 2, dc in same st as joining, dc in next st, 2 dc in next st, [dc in each of next 2 sts, 2 dc in next st] 8 times; join with sl st to first dc. (36 dc)

Round 4: Ch 2, dc in each st around; join with sl st to first dc. (36 dc)

Round 5: Ch 2, dc in same st as joining, dc in each of next 2 sts, 2 dc in next st, [dc in each of next 3 sts, 2 dc in next st] 8 times; join with sl st to first dc. (45 dc)

Rounds 6-17: *(12 rounds)* Ch 2, dc in each st around; join with sl st to first dc. (45 dc)
At the end of Round 17, fasten off with a Needle Join.

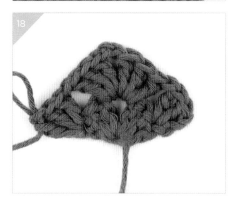

Dress Collar

Row 1: Holding the Doll right side up, working in the unused front loops on Round 1 of Dress, attach **Color D** to st at center front; *(image 14)* ch 2, 3 dc in next st, [dc in next st, 2 dc in next st] 7 times, dc in next st, 3 dc in next st, sc in next st. (28 dc & 1 sc)

Row 2: Ch 1, turn, skip first sc, [sc in each of next 2 sts, inc in next st] across, ending with sc in last dc. (37 sc) Fasten off and weave in all ends.

- Position the Arms on either side of the Body under the Dress Collar, and sew in place. *(image 15)*

HAIR

Round 1: With **Color B**, make a magic ring, 6 sc in ring. (6 sc) Tug tail to tighten ring. Do not join. Mark last st made. Move marker at the end of each round.

Round 2: Inc in each st around. (12 sc)

Round 3: [Sc in next st, inc in next st] 6 times. (18 sc)

Round 4: [Sc in each of next 2 sts, inc in next st] 6 times. (24 sc)

Round 5: [Sc in each of next 3 sts, inc in next st] 6 times. (30 sc)

Round 6: [Sc in each of next 4 sts, inc in next st] 6 times. (36 sc)

Round 7: [Sc in each of next 5 sts, inc in next st] 6 times. (42 sc)

Round 8: [Sc in each of next 6 sts, inc in next st] 6 times. (48 sc)

Round 9: [Sc in each of next 7 sts, inc in next st] 6 times. (54 sc)

Round 10: [Sc in each of next 8 sts, inc in next st] 3 times, sc in each of next 27 sts. (57 sc)

Rounds 11-20: *(10 rounds)* Sc in each st around. (57 sc)

Round 21: Sc in each of next 32 sts, hdc in each of next 2 sts, dc in next st, 2 dc in next st, hdc in each of next 2 sts, sc in each of next 2 sts, hdc in next st, dc in each of next 2 sts, [2 dc in next st, dc in each of next 2 sts] 2 times, hdc in each of next 2 sts, sc in each of next 5 sts, sl st in next st. Fasten off, leaving a long tail for sewing.

Hair Bun

Rounds 1-7: Repeat rounds 1-7 of Hair.

Rounds 8-11: *(4 rounds)* Sc in each st around. (42 sc)

Round 12: [Sc in each of next 5 sts, dec] 6 times. (36 sc) Fasten off, leaving a long tail for sewing.

- Position the Hair on head, with the "parting" to one side, and sew in place.

- Stuff the Hair Bun lightly, position on top of Head, and sew in place.

- Sew a stitch or two through the center of the Bun to the Head, pulling tightly to make an indentation. Secure with a knot and weave in ends. *(image 16)*

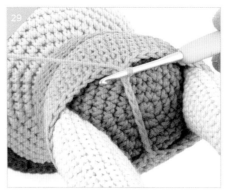

SHAWL

Row 1: With **Color C**, ch 3, (2 dc, ch 2, 3 dc) in 3rd ch from hook *(skipped ch-2 counts as first dc)*. (6 dc & corner ch-2 sp) *(image 17)*

Row 2: Ch 2 *(counts as first dc, now and throughout)*, turn, 2 dc in first st, ch 1, skip next 2 sts, (3 dc, ch 2, 3 dc) in next ch-2 sp, ch 1, skip next 2 sts, 3 dc in last st. (12 dc, 2 ch-1 sps & corner ch-2 sp) *(image 18)*

Row 3: Ch 2, turn, 2 dc in first st, ch 1, skip next 2 sts, 3 dc in next ch-1 sp, ch 1, (3 dc, ch 2, 3 dc) in next ch-2 sp, ch 1, 3 dc in next ch-1 sp, ch 1, skip next 2 sts, 3 dc in last st. (18 dc, 4 ch-1 sps & corner ch-2 sp)

Rows 4-10: Ch 2, turn, 2 dc in first st, ch 1, skip next 2 sts, [3 dc in next ch-1 sp, ch 1] across to corner, (3 dc, ch 2, 3 dc) in next ch-2 sp, [ch 1, 3 dc in next ch-1 sp] across, ending with ch 1, skip next 2 sts, 3 dc in last st.
At the end of Row 10, fasten off leaving a long tail for sewing. *(image 19)*

- Wrap the Shawl around Grandma's shoulders and using the long tail, sew the two corners together. Weave in all ends.

GRANDPA

HAIR

Row 1: With **Color B**, ch 35, starting in 3rd ch from hook, dc in each ch across. (33 dc)

Row 2: Ch 2, turn, working in the sps between the sts, hdc in each st across. (33 hdc) *(image 20)*

Row 3: Ch 2, turn, dc in each st across. (33 dc)

Row 4: Ch 2, turn, [dc in each of next 5 sts, dec] 4 times, dc in each of next 5 sts. (29 dc) Fasten off, leaving a long tail for sewing.

- Position the Hair on the back of the Head, and sew in place.

PANTS

Round 1: Holding the Doll upside down, working in the unused front loops on Round 10 on Body, attach **Color F** to stitch at center back, *(image 21-22)* ch 1, sc in same st, sc in each of next 8 sts, inc in next st, sc in each of next 22 sts, inc in next st, sc in each of next 9 sts; join with sl st to first st. (44 sc)

Rounds 2-6: Ch 1, sc in each st around; join with sl st to first st. (44 sc)
At the end of Round 6, continue with First Leg.

First Leg

Round 1: Ch 8, skip next 22 st, sc in each of next 22 sts; *(image 23-24)* working in ch-8, sc in each of next 8 ch; join with sl st to first st. (30 sc)

Round 2: Ch 1, sc in each of next 20 sts, dec, sc in each of next 6 sts, dec; join with sl st to first st. (28 sc)

Round 3: Ch 1, sc in each of next 18 sts, dec, sc in each of next 6 sts, dec; join with sl st to first st. (26 sc)

Round 4: Ch 1, sc in each of next 18 sts, dec, sc in each of next 4 sts, dec; join with sl st to first st. (24 sc)

Rounds 5-19: *(15 rounds)* Ch 1, sc in each st around; join with sl st to first st. (24 sc)
At the end of Round 19, fasten off and weave in ends. *(image 25)*

Second Leg

Round 1: Working on other side of ch-8, attach **Color F** to first ch, ch 1, sc in same ch, sc in each of next 7 ch, working in skipped sts, sc in each of next 22 sts. (30 sc) *(image 26-27)*

Round 2: Ch 1, sc in each of next 6 sts, dec, sc in each of next 20 sts, dec; join with sl st to first st. (28 sc)

Round 3: Ch 1, sc in each of next 6 sts, dec, sc in each of next 18 sts, dec; join with sl st to first st. (26 sc)

Round 4: Ch 1, sc in each of next 4 sts, dec, sc in each of next 18 sts, dec; join with sl st to first st. (24 sc)

Rounds 5-18: *(14 rounds)* Ch 1, sc in each st around; join with sl st to first st. (24 sc)
At the end of Round 18, fasten off and weave in ends.

Shirt Collar

Row 1: Holding the Doll right side up, working in the unused front loops on Round 24 of Body, attach **Color E** to st at center front; *(image 28)* ch 2, 3 dc in next st, [dc in next st, 2 dc in next st] 7 times, dc in next st, 3 dc in next st, sl st in next st. (28 dc & 1 sl st) Fasten off and weave in all ends.

- Position the Arms on either side of the Body under the Shirt Collar, and sew in place.

VEST

Row 1: With **Color C**, ch 47; starting from 3rd ch from hook (skipped *ch-sts count as first dc*), dc in each ch across. (46 dc)

Rows 2-3: Ch 2 *(counts as first dc, now and throughout)*, turn, dc in each st across. (46 dc)

Row 4: Ch 2, turn, dc in each of next 3 sts, [dc2tog, dc in each of next 5 sts] 6 times. (40 dc)

Row 5: Ch 2, turn, dc in each of next 4 sts, [dc2tog, dc in each of next 5 sts] 5 times. (35 dc)

Row 6: Ch 2, turn, dc in each of next 6 sts, [dc2tog, dc in each of next 5 sts] 4 times. (31 dc)

First Shoulder

Row 1: Ch 2, turn, dc in each of next 3 sts. (4 dc) Leave remaining sts unworked.

Rows 2-4: Ch 2, turn, dc in each st across. (4 dc) At the end of Row 4, fasten off, leaving a long tail for sewing.

Center Back

Row 1: Working in Row 6, skip next 4 sts, attach Color C to next st, ch 2, dc in each of next 14 sts. (15 dc) Leave remaining sts unworked. Fasten off.

Second Shoulder

Row 1: Working in Row 6, skip next 4 sts, attach Color C to next st, ch 2, dc in each of next 3 sts. (4 dc)

Rows 2-4: Ch 2, turn, dc in each st across. (4 dc) At the end of Row 4, fasten off, leaving a long tail for sewing. *(image 29)*

- Fold the Vest into shape, and using the long tails, sew the Shoulders to the outer stitches on Center Back. *(image 30)*

- Place Vest on Grandpa.

FINISHING THE DOLLS

- Position Ears on either side of Head between Rounds 38 & 39 and sew in place.

- Using Black Floss, embroider the Eyes between Rounds 38 & 39, with 7 stitches between them.

- With **MC**, embroider the Nose between the Eyes and one round below them, using a few horizontal straight stitches over about 3-4 stitches.

- With **MC**, embroider a small Mouth, about 2 rounds below the Nose.

- Using **Color B**, embroider Eyebrows 3-4 rounds above Eyes.

- Apply Blusher to cheeks.

For Grandpa

- With **Color B**, embroider a moustache under the Nose.

- With **Color F**, embroider about 6 Buttons down center front of Shirt.

grany and her Little Helper

designer

Kate and Dasha

@grannyscrochethook

Materials & Tools

HELLO Cotton Yarn

For Granny

» **Main Color (MC):** (158) Dark Beige - for Head, Legs & Arms

» **Color A:** Brown (126) - for Shoes

» **Color B:** White (154) - for Bloomers & Apron

» **Color C:** Off-White (155) - for Hair

» **Color D:** Fuchsia (106) - for Skirt

For Helper

» **Main Color (MC):** Dark Beige (158) - for Body

» **Color A:** Brown (126) - for Shoes & Hair

» **Color B:** White (154) - for Hat, Bib & Gloves

» **Color E:** Gray Blue (149) - for Pants

» **Color F:** Chartreuse (130) - for Shirt

For Cake

» **Color A:** Brown (126)

» **Color B:** White (154)

» **Color G:** Salmon (109)

» **Color H:** Magenta (107)

Hook Size

» 2.5 mm hook

Other

» Stitch Markers

» Yarn Needle

» Stuffing

» DMC Embroidery Floss – Black & Pink (for facial features)

» Embroidery Needle

» Water Soluble Marker

» Straight Pins

» Tiny Buttons - to decorate clothes (2 for Granny)

» Sewing thread & Needle (for Buttons)

» Toy Eyeglasses or

To Make Your Own Eyeglasses (Optional):

» 8" (20 cm) length of crafting wire

» Cylinder shape of desired size

» Pliers – to bend and cut the wire.

» Small piece cardboard – for Cake structure

» Optional (but recommended)

» Flat Buttons x 2 – for each Doll.

(These are put in the base of the Legs to keep the soles flat. Alternatively, you can use a piece of cardboard cut to fit.)

Finished Size

Granny - About 9¾" (25 cm) tall
Little Helper - About 7½" (19 cm) tall
Cake - About 2¾" (7 cm) high

Skill Level

Intermediate

SPECIAL STITCHES & TECHNIQUES

Single Crochet Spike Stitch (sc-sp)

Insert hook in corresponding stitch one round below the working round and pull up a loop to the height of a single crochet stitch *(two loops on hook)*. Yarn over, and draw through both loops on hook.

Note: *The Spike Stitch is worked exactly like a regular basic crochet stitch, except the hook is inserted one or more rounds below the working round.*

Bobble with 5 Double Crochet (bob)

Yarn over, insert hook in stitch or space specified and draw up a loop *(3 loops on hook)*, yarn over and draw through two loops on hook *(2 loops remain)*, *yarn over and insert hook in same stitch or space and draw up a loop, yarn over and draw through two loops on hook; repeat from * 3 times more *(6 loops on hook)*; yarn over and draw through all six loops; ch 1 *(to secure)*. Bobble made.

Double Crochet Decrease (dc2tog)

Yarn over hook, insert hook in stitch or space specified and pull up a loop *(3 loops on hook)*; yarn over and draw through 2 loops on hook *(2 loops remain)*; yarn over hook, insert hook in next the stitch or space and pull up a loop *(4 loops on hook)*; yarn over and draw through 2 loops on hook *(3 loops remain)*; yarn over and draw through all 3 loops on hook. Decrease made.

To Make Eyeglasses (Optional)

Wrap a piece of crafting wire around a cylindrical object of the desired size (we used the handle of a wooden spoon). Then leave a small section (the distance between the eyes) and wrap the wire again. Using pliers, bend the wire 90° to make the sidepieces. Trim the excess wire.

Reverse Single Crochet (r-sc)

Working from left to right, *insert hook in next stitch to the right and pull up a loop *(2 loops on hook)*; yarn over and draw through both loops on hook; repeat from * across or around, as instructed.

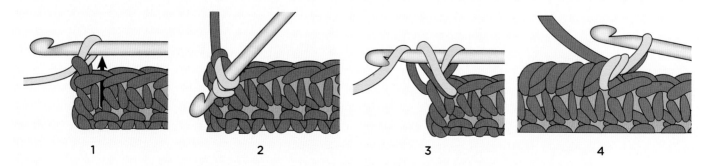

1   2   3   4

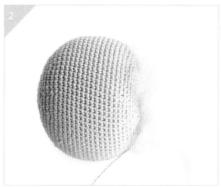

GRANNY

HEAD

Round 1: With **MC**, make a magic ring; 6 sc in ring. (6 sc) Tug tail to tighten ring. Do not join. Mark last st. Move marker at the end of each round.

Round 2: Inc in each st around. (12 sc)

Round 3: [Sc in next st, inc in next st] 6 times. (18 sc)

Round 4: Sc in next st, inc in next st, [sc in each of next 2 sts, inc in next st] 5 times, sc in next st. (24 sc)

Round 5: [Sc in each of next 3 sts, inc in next st] 6 times. (30 sc)

Round 6: Sc in each of next 2 sts, inc in next st, [sc in each of next 4 sts, inc in next st] 5 times, sc in each of next 2 sts. (36 sc)

Round 7: [Sc in each of next 5 sts, inc in next st] 6 times. (42 sc)

Round 8: Sc in each of next 3 sts, inc in next st, [sc in each of next 6 sts, inc in next st] 5 times, sc in each of next 3 sts. (48 sc)

Round 9: [Sc in each of next 7 sts, inc in next st] 6 times. (54 sc)

Round 10: Sc in each of next 4 sts, inc in next st, [sc in each of next 8 sts, inc in next st] 5 times, sc in each of next 4 sts. (60 sc)

Round 11: [Sc in each of next 9 sts, inc in next st] 6 times. (66 sc)

Rounds 12-25: *(14 rounds)* Sc in each st around. (66 sc)

Round 26: [Sc in each of next 9 sts, dec] 6 times. (60 sc)

Round 27: Sc in each of next 4 sts, dec, [sc in each of next 8 sts, dec] 5 times, sc in each of next 4 sts. (54 sc)

Round 28: [Sc in each of next 7 sts, dec] 6 times. (48 sc)

Round 29: Sc in each of next 3 sts, dec, [sc in each of next 6 sts, dec] 5 times, sc in each of next 3 sts. (42 sc)

Round 30: [Sc in each of next 5 sts, dec] 6 times. (36 sc) Sl st in next st. Fasten off and weave in all ends.

- Stuff the Head firmly. *(image 1-3)*

LEG (Make 2)

Rounds 1-3: Using **Color A**, repeat Rounds 1-3 of the Head.

Round 4: Working in **back loops** only, sc in each st around. (18 sc)

Round 5: Sc in each st around, changing to **MC** in last st. (18 sc)

Round 6: With **MC**, working in **back loops** only, sl st in each st around. (18 sl sts)

- Place a button or cardboard circle in the base of the Leg. (This is optional, but highly recommended as it helps keep the foot flat and makes it look nice.) *(fotoğraf 4-5)*

Round 7: Working in **back loops** only, sc in each sl st around. (18 sc)

Rounds 8-17: *(10 rounds)* Sc in each st around. (18 sc)

At the end of Round 17, change to **Color B** in last st.

- Stuff the lower part of the Leg firmly, adding more as you go.

Round 18: With **Color B**, working in **back loops** only, sc in each st around. (18 sc)

Round 19: Sc-sp in each st *(same back loop on Round 17)* around. (18 sc)

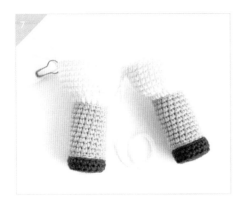
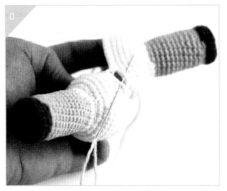

Round 20: Working in **back loops** only, inc in each st around. (36 sc)

Rounds 21-25: *(5 rounds)* Sc in each st around. (36 sc) At the end of Round 25, for the First Leg, fasten off leaving a long tail for closing the gap between the Legs. *(image 6)*

For the Second Leg, do not fasten off. Continue with Body.

BODY

Round 1: *(Joining Legs)* Working on First Leg, sl st in 4th st, sc in each of next 32 sts *(leave remaining 3 sts unworked)*; working on Second Leg, skip first 3 sts, sl st in 4th st, sc in each of next 17 sts. Leave remaining sts unworked. Mark last st as new end of round. *(image 7)* Move marker at the end of each round.

Round 2: Sc in each st around. (66 sc) *(image 8-10)*

 - Using the First Leg's long tail and yarn needle, close the gap between the Legs securely and weave in the end.

Rounds 3-17: *(15 rounds)* Sc in each st around. (66 sc) *(image 11)*

 - Start stuffing Body, adding more as you go.

Round 18: [Sc in each of next 9 sts, dec] 6 times. (60 sc)

Round 19: Sc in each st around. (60 sc)

 - Sc across to side of Body (1 or 2 sts), changing to **Color D** in last st. Mark last st as new end of round. Move marker at the end of each round.

Round 20: With **Color D**, sc in each of next 4 sts, dec, [sc in each of next 8 sts, dec] 5 times, sc in each of next 4 sts, changing to **Color B** in last st. (54 sc) Leave **Color D** hanging on the inside.

Round 21: With **Color B**, working in **back loops** only, sc in each st around. (54 sc) *(image 12)*

Round 22: Sc-sp in each st *(same back loop on Round 20)* around, changing to **Color D** in last st. (54 sc)

Round 23: With **Color D**, working in **back loops** only, sc in each st around. (54 sc)

Round 24: [Sc in each of next 7 sts, dec] 6 times. (48 sc)

Round 25: Sc in each st around. (48 sc)

Round 26: Sc in each of next 3 sts, dec, [sc in each of next 6 sts, dec] 5 times, sc in each of next 3 sts. (42 sc)

Round 27: Sc in each st around. (42 sc)

Round 28: [Sc in each of next 5 sts, dec] 6 times, changing to **Color B** in last st. (36 sc) Fasten off **Color D**.

Round 29: With **Color B**, working in **back loops** only, sc in each st around. (36 sc)

Round 30: Sc-sp in each st *(same back loop on Round 28)* around, changing to **MC** in last st. (36 sc) Fasten off **Color B**.

Round 31: With **MC**, working in **back loops** only, sc in each st around. (36 sc) Fasten off, leaving a long tail for sewing.

 - Stuff the Body firmly. *(image 13)*

ARM (Make 2)

Round 1: With **MC**, make a magic ring; 6 sc in ring. (6 sc) Tug tail to tighten ring. Do not join. Mark last st. Move marker at the end of each round.

Round 2: Inc in each st around. (12 sc)

Round 3: Sc in each st around. (12 sc)

Round 4: Sc in each of next 5 sts, **bob** in **front loop** only of next st, sc in each of next 6 sts. (12 sc)

- Start stuffing the Arm firmly, adding more as you go.

Rounds 5-15: *(11 rounds)* Sc in each st around. (12 sc)
At the end of Round 15, change to **Color B** in last st. Fasten off **MC**.

Round 16: With **Color B**, working in **back loops** only, sc in each st around. (12 sc)

Round 17: Sc-sp in each st *(same back loop on Round 15)* around, changing to **Color D** in last st. Fasten off **Color B**.

Round 18: With **Color D**, working in **back loops** only, inc in each st around. (24 sc)

Round 19: [Sc in each of next 3 sts, inc in next st] 6 times. (30 sc)

Rounds 20-21: *(2 rounds)* Sc in each st around. (30 sc)

Round 22: Sc in each of next 4 sts, dec, [sc in each of next 8 sts, dec] 2 times, sc in each of next 4 sts. (27 sc)

- Start stuffing the Sleeve lightly, adding more as you go.

Round 23: [Sc in each of next 7 sts, dec] 3 times. (24 sc)

Round 24: Sc in each of next 3 sts, dec, [sc in each of next 6 sts, dec] 2 times, sc in each of next 3 sts. (21 sc)

Round 25: [Sc in each of next 5 sts, dec] 3 times. (18 sc)

Round 26: Sc in each of next 2 sts, dec, [sc in each of next 4 sts, dec] 2 times, sc in each of next 2 sts. (15 sc)

Round 27: [Sc in each of next 3 sts, dec] 3 times. (12 sc)

- Finish stuffing the Sleeve lightly.

Last row: Flatten the last round and working through both thicknesses, sc in each of next 6 sts. Fasten off, leaving a long tail for sewing. *(image 14)*

SKIRT

Notes:

1. Should you prefer to make the skirt more voluminous, you may use a slightly larger size hook.

2. We make the skirt as a separate piece and sew it onto the Body, but if you prefer, you may work Round 1 directly onto the Body, by working a single crochet stitch in each of the unused front loops of Round 20.

Round 1: With **Color D**, ch 54; taking care not to twist chain, sl st in first ch to form a ring; sc in each ch around. (54 sc) Do not join. Mark last st. Move marker at the end of each round.

Round 2: Sc in each of next 4 sts, inc in next st, [sc in each of next 8 sts, inc in next st] 5 times, sc in each of next 4 sts. (60 sc)

Round 3: [Sc in each of next 9 sts, inc in next st] 6 times. (66 sc)

Rounds 4-6: *(3 rounds)* Sc in each st around. (66 sc)

Round 7: Sc in each of next 5 sts, inc in next st, [sc in each of next 10 sts, inc in next st] 5 times, sc in each of next 5 sts. (72 sc)

Rounds 8-15: *(8 rounds)* Sc in each st around. (72 sc)

Round 16: [Sc in each of next 11 sts, inc in next st] 6 times. (78 sc)

Rounds 17-23: *(7 rounds)* Sc in each st around. (78 sc) At the end of Round 23, change to **Color B** in last st. Leave **Color D** hanging on the inside.

Round 24: With **Color B**, working in **back loops** only, sc in each st around. (78 sc)

Round 25: Sc-sp in each st *(same back loop on Round 23)* around, changing to **Color D** in last st. Fasten off **Color B**.

Round 26: With **Color D**, working in **back loops** only, sc in each st around. (78 sc) Fasten off with Needle Join and weave in ends. *(image 15)*

NOSE

Round 1: With **MC**, make a magic ring; 6 sc in ring. (6 sc) Tug tail to tighten ring. Do not join.

Round 2: Sc in each st around. (6sc) Fasten off, leaving long tail for sewing.

HAIR

Base Cap

Note: *The Base Cap can be made using another similar color (for example, MC, if you have leftovers) as it's going to be completely covered with Curls.*

Round 1: With **Color C**, make a magic ring; 8 sc in ring. (8 sc) Tug tail to tighten ring. Do not join. Mark last st. Move marker at the end of each round.

Round 2: Working in **back loops** only, 2 dc in each st around. (16 dc)

Round 3: Working in **back loops** only,

2 dc in each st around. (32 dc)

Round 4: Working in **back loops** only, [2 dc in next st, dc in next st] 16 times. (48 dc)

Round 5: Working in **back loops** only, [2 dc in next st, dc in each of next 7 sts] 6 times. (54 dc)

Rounds 6-10: *(5 rounds)* Working in **back loops** only, dc in each st around. (54 dc)

Round 11: Working in **back loops** only, [**dc2tog**, dc in each of next 7 sts] 5 times, dc2tog, dc in each of next 3 sts, hdc in each of next 2 sts, sc in next st, sl st in next st. (48 sts) Do not fasten off. Continue with Curls. *(image 16-17)*

Note: Don't worry if the Base Cap is a little bit tight on the Head. It will expand when making the Curls.

Curls

Note: Crochet the Curls loosely or if you prefer, use a slightly larger size hook.

Spiral Rounds: Ch 2, turn, working in unused front loops of Rounds 10 to 1, 4 dc in each st around. Fasten off, and weave in ends. *(image 18-23)*

APRON

Row 1: With **Color B,** ch 8; starting in 3rd ch from hook, hdc in each of next 5 ch, 6 hdc in last ch; working on other side of starting chain, hdc in each of next 5 ch. (16 hdc)

Row 2: Ch 2, turn, hdc in first st, hdc in each of next 4 sts, 2 hdc in each of next 6 sts, hdc in each of next 5 sts. (22 hdc)

Row 3: Ch 2, turn, hdc in first st, hdc in each of next 5 sts, [2 hdc in next st, hdc in next st] 6 times, hdc in each of next 4 sts. (28 hdc)

Row 4: Ch 2, turn, hdc in first st, hdc in each of next 5 sts, [2 hdc in next st, hdc in each of next 2 sts] 5 times, 2 hdc in next st, hdc in each of next 6 sts. (34 hdc)

Row 5: Ch 1, turn, sc in first st, [skip next st, 5 hdc in next st, skip next st, sl st in next st] 8 times, sc in last st. (50 sts) Fasten off, weaving in ends. *(image 24)*

Bow

With **Color B,** leaving a 6" (15 cm) long tail, [ch 33; starting in 2nd ch from hook, sl st in each of next 32 ch] 2 times. Fasten off, leaving another 6" (15 cm) tail.

- Shape each end to form a bow, wrapping the yarn tails around the center to hold the shape. Secure with a knot, leaving a tail for sewing. *(image 25)*

ASSEMBLY AND FINISHING TOUCHES (use photos as guide)

Skirt - Position the Skirt on the Body. Using a strand of **Color D,** sew the unused loops of the starting chain to the unworked front loops of Round 20. *(image 26)*

Head - Using the long tail of the Body, position and sew the Head to the Body, matching stitch for stitch. *(image 27)*

Arms - Position the Arms on either side of the Body, between Rounds 27 and 28. Using long tails and yarn needle, sew them in place. *(image 28)*

Hair - Place the Hair on the Head (at approximately a 45° angle) and secure it in place with straight pins. Using a long strand of **Color C,** sew the Hair to Head by making stitches in between the rounds. *(image 29)*

Apron - Position the Apron to the center front of Skirt. Using a single strand of **Color B,** sew the top of the Apron to Round 1 of the Skirt. *(image 30)*

- Place the Bow at center back of Doll, just above the Skirt. Using the yarn tails, sew in place. *(image 31)*

Buttons - Sew the Buttons to the front of the Body, between Rounds 24 and 27.

Knees - Using a strand of **MC** and yarn needle, embroider about 2-3 horizontal stitches (over 3 sc) between Rounds 13 & 14 at the center front of each Leg. *(image 32)*

Face - Use the diagram as a guide.

- Mark the position of the Eyes and Mouth using a water-soluble marker (or straight pins), finding the option that looks good to you.

- Position the Nose in the center of the face between the 4th & 7th round from Hairline. Split the yarn tail into 2 strands, and using one strand and sewing needle, sew in place. Hide the second strand in the Head.

- Using Black Floss, embroider the Eyes.

- Using a single strand of **Color A,** embroider the Mouth.

- Using **Color B,** embroider the Eyebrows.

- With Pink Floss, embroider the Cheeks using horizontal straight stitches. *(image 33-34)*

- Place Eyeglasses on Face.

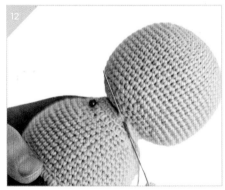
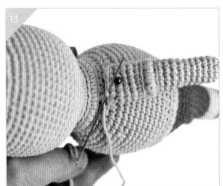

GRANNY'S LITTLE HELPER

HEAD

Rounds 1-9: Repeat Rounds 1-9 of Granny Head.

Rounds 10-21: *(12 rounds)* Sc in each st around. (54 sc)

Round 22: [Sc in each of next 7 sts, dec] 6 times. (48 sc)

Round 23: Sc in each of next 3 sts, dec, [sc in each of next 6 sts, dec] 5 times, sc in each of next 3 sts. (42 sc)

Round 24: [Sc in each of next 5 sts, dec] 6 times. (36 sc)

Round 25: Sc in each of next 2 sts, dec, [sc in each of next 4 sts, dec] 5 times, sc in next st, sl st in next st. (30 sts) Fasten off and weave in all ends.

- Stuff the Head firmly. *(image 1)*

LEG (Make 2)

Rounds 1: With **Color A**, make a magic ring; 8 sc in ring. (8 sc) Tug tail to tighten ring. Do not join. Mark last st. Move marker at the end of each round.

Round 2: Inc in each st around. (16 sc)

Round 3: Working in **back loops** only, sc in each st around. (16 sc)

Round 4: Sc in each st around, changing to **MC** in last st. (16 sc)

Round 5: With **MC**, working in **back loops** only, sl st in each st around. (16 sl sts)

Round 6: Working in **back loops** only, sc in each sl st around. (16 sc)

- Place a button or cardboard circle in the base of the Leg. (This is optional, but highly recommended as it helps keep the foot flat and makes it look nice.) *(image 2)*

Rounds 7-10: *(4 rounds)* Sc in each st around. (16 sc) At the end of Round 10, change to **Color E** in last st.

Round 11: Working in **back loops** only, sl st in each st around. (16 sl sts)

Round 12: Working in **back loops** only, sc in each sl st around. (16 sc)

Rounds 13-15: *(3 rounds)* Sc in each st around. (16 sc) At the end of Round 15, for the First Leg, fasten off and weave in ends. *(image 3)* For the Second Leg, do not fasten off. Continue with Body.

BODY

Round 1: *(Joining Legs)* Ch 5; working on First Leg, sl st in first st, sc in each of next 15 sts; working in ch-5, sc in each of next 5 ch; working on Second Leg, sc in each of next 16 sts; working on other side of ch-5, sc in each of next 5 ch. (42 sts) Sc in each of next 8 sts to move the end of round to side of the body. Mark the last stitch. *(image 4)* Move the marker each round.

Round 2: Sc in each of next 3 sts, inc in next st, [sc in each of next 6 sts, inc in next st] 5 times, sc in each of next 3 sts. (48 sc)

Round 3: [Sc in each of next 7 sts, inc in next st] 6 times. (54 sc)

- Stuff the Legs firmly. Start stuffing the Body, adding more as you go.

Rounds 4-8: *(5 rounds)* Sc in each st around. (54 sc) At the end of Round 8, change to **Color F**.

Round 9: With **Color F**, working in **back loops** only, sc in each st around. (54 sc)

Round 10: Sc-sp in each st *(same back loop on Round 8)* around. (54 sc) *(image 5)*

Round 11: Working in **back loops** only, sc in each st around. (54 sc)

Rounds 12-17: *(6 rounds)* Sc in each st around. (54 sc)

Round 18: [Sc in each of next 7 sts, dec] 6 times. (48 sc)

Rounds 19-20: *(2 rounds)* Sc in each st around. (48 sc)

Round 21: Sc in each of next 3 sts, dec, [sc in each of next 6 sts, dec] 5 times, sc in each of next 3 sts. (42 sc)

Round 22: [Sc in each of next 5 sts, dec] 6 times. (36 sc)

Round 23: Sc in each of next 2 sts, dec, [sc in each of next 4 sts, dec] 5 times, sc in each of next 2 sts. (30 sc)

Round 24: Working in **back loops** only, sc in each st around. (30 sc)

Round 25: Sc-sp in each st *(same back loop on Round 23)* around, changing to **MC** in last st.. (30 sc)

Round 26: With **MC**, working in **back loops** only, sc in each of next 29 sts, sl st in next st. (30 sts) Fasten off, leaving a long tail for sewing. *(image 6)*

ARM (Make 2)

Round 1: With **MC**, make a magic ring; 5 sc in ring. (5 sc) Tug tail to tighten ring. Do not join. Mark last st. Move marker at the end of each round.

Round 2: Inc in each st around. (10 sc)

Rounds 3-8: *(6 rounds)* Sc in each st around. (10 sc)

Round 9: [Inc in next st, sc in each of next 4 sts] 2 times. (12 sc)

Rounds 10-12: *(3 rounds)* Sc in each st around. (12 sc) At the end of the Round 12, change to **Color F.**

Round 13: With **Color F**, working in **back loops** only, sc in each st around. (12 sc)

Round 14: Sc-sp in each st *(same back loop on Round 12)* around. (12 sc)

Round 15: Working in **back loops** only, sc in each st around. (12 sc)

Rounds 16-18: *(3 rounds)* Sc in each st around. (12 sc)

 - Stuff the bottom of the Arm.

Last Row: Flatten the last round and working through both thicknesses, sc in each of next 6 sts. Fasten off, leaving a long tail for sewing. *(image 7)*

HAIR

Rounds 1-10: With **Color A**, repeat Rounds 1-10 of Granny Head.

Round 11: Sc in each st around. (60 sc)

Rounds 12-19: *(8 rounds)* Hdc in each of next 17 sts, sc in next st, sl st in next st, sc in next st, hdc in each of next 13 sts, sc in each of next 27 sts. (60 sts)

Last Row: Sc in each of next 2 sts, hdc in each of next 13 sts, sc in each of next 3 sc, sl st in next st (19 sts). Leave remaining sts unworked. Fasten off, leaving a long tail for making the Hair parting. *(image 8-9)*

Hair Tufts

Leaving a 4" (10 cm) tail, ch 9; starting in 2nd ch from hook, sl st in each of next 8 ch; ch 7, starting in 2nd ch from hook, sl st in each of next 6 ch. Fasten off, leaving another long tail for sewing. *(image 10)*

NOSE

Round 1: With **MC**, make a magic ring; 5 sc in ring. (5 sc) Tug tail to tighten ring. Do not join.

Round 2: Sc in each st around. (5 sc) Sl st in next st. Fasten off, leaving long tail for sewing.

EAR (Make 2)

With **MC**, make a Magic Ring; 8 sc in ring; tug tail to tighten ring; join with sl st to first sc. (8 sc) Fasten off, leaving a long tail for sewing.

KITCHEN GLOVE (Make 2)

Note: *Crochet loosely to make the gloves softer.*

Round 1: With **Color B,** make a magic ring; 8 sc in ring. (8 sc) Tug tail to tighten ring. Do not join. Mark last st. Move marker at the end of each round.

Round 2: Inc in each st around. (16 sc)

Round 3: Sc in each st around. (16 sc)

Round 4: Sc in each of next 7 sts, **bob** in next st, sc in each of next 8 sts. (16 sc)

Rounds 5-9: *(5 rounds)* Sc in each st around. (16 sc)

Round 10: Sl st in each st around. (16 sl ts) Fasten off, weaving in ends.

BIB

Row 1: With **Color B**, ch 8; starting in 3rd ch from hook, hdc in each of next 5 ch, 6 hdc in last ch; working on other side

of starting chain, hdc in each of next 5 ch. (16 hdc)

Row 2: Ch 2, turn, hdc in first st, hdc in each of next 4 sts, 2 hdc in each of next 6 sts, hdc in each of next 5 sts. (22 hdc)

Row 3: Ch 2, turn, hdc in first st, hdc in each of next 5 sts, [2 hdc in next st, hdc in next st] 6 times, hdc in each of next 4 sts. (28 hdc)

Row 4: Ch 1, turn, sc in first st, sc in each of next 5 sts, inc in next st, [sc in each of next 2 sts, inc in next st] 5 times, sc in each of next 6 sc. (34 sc)

Last Row: *(Ties)* Ch 26; starting in 2nd ch from hook, sl st in each of the 25 ch, working in ends of rows, work 12 sc evenly across to end; ch 26; starting in 2nd ch from hook, sl st in each of the 25 ch. Fasten off, and weave in ends.

CHEF'S HAT

Round 1: With **Color B**, make a magic ring; 6 sc in ring. (6 sc) Tug tail to tighten ring. Do not join. Mark last st. Move marker at the end of each round.

Round 2: Inc in each st around. (12 sc)

Round 3: [Sc in next st, inc in next st] 6 times. (18 sc)

Round 4: Sc in next st, inc in next st, [sc in each of next 2 sts, inc in next st] 5 times, sc in next st. (24 sc)

Round 5: [Sc in each of next 3 sts, inc in next st] 6 times. (30 sc)

Round 6: Sc in each of next 2 sts, inc in next st, [sc in each of next 4 sts, inc in next st] 5 times, sc in each of next 2 sts. (36 sc)

Round 7: [Sc in each of next 5 sts, inc in next st] 6 times. (42 sc)

Round 8: Sc in each of next 3 sts, inc in next st, [sc in each of next 6 sts, inc in next st] 5 times, sc in each of next 3 sts. (48 sc)

Round 9: [Sc in each of next 7 sts, inc in next st] 6 times. (54 sc)

Round 10: Sc in each of next 4 sts, inc in next st, [sc in each of next 8 sts, inc in next st] 5 times, sc in each of next 4 sts. (60 sc)

Rounds 11-13: *(3 rounds)* Sc in each st around. (60 sc)

Round 14: [Dec] 30 times. (30 sc)

Rounds 15-18: *(4 rounds)* Sc in each st around. (30 sc)

Round 19: Sl st in each st around. (30 sl sts) Fasten off, weaving in ends.

ASSEMBLY AND FINISHING TOUCHES (use photos as guide)

Head - Using the long tail of the Body, position and sew the Head to the Body, matching stitch for stitch. *(image 12)*

Arms - Position the Arms on either side of the Body,

between Rounds 22 and 23. Using long tails and yarn needle, sew them in place. *(image 13)*

Hair

- Place the Hair on the Head (at approximately a 45° angle) and secure it in place with straight pins. *(image 13)*

- Using the yarn tails, sew the Hair Tufts to the Head through the center of Hair (at magic ring).

- Pin out the shape of the hair parting, and using the long tail, starting from the outer edge and working to the Hair Tufts, sew the parting through the Hair and Head using small back stitches. *(image 15)*

- Add a bit of stuffing under the Hair on either side of the parting. (Make sure the Helper's hair looks nice and even, and has the shape of an apple.)

- Using a single strand of **Color A**, sew the Hair to the Head neatly around the perimeter. *(image 16)*

Ears - Position the Ears on either side of the Head, just under the edge of the Hair. Using long tails and yarn needle, sew them in place. *(image 17)*

Face - Use the diagram as a guide.

- Mark the position of the Eyes and Mouth using a water-soluble marker (or straight pins), finding the option that looks good to you.

- Position the Nose in the center of the face between the 4th & 7th round from Hairline. Split the yarn tail into 2 strands, and using one strand and sewing needle, sew in place. Hide the second strand in the Head.

- Using Black Floss, embroider the Eyes.

- Using a single strand of **Color A,** embroider the Mouth.

- Using **Color A**, embroider the Eyebrows.

- With Pink Floss, embroider the Cheeks using horizontal straight stitches.

- With **Color B**, embroider the Teeth. *(image 18)*

Accessories

- Place the Bib on the Helper, tying the ties at the back of the neck.

- Position the Chef's Hat on top of the Hair and sew in place. (Or if you want it removable, make ties out of a piece of yarn.)

- Place the Gloves on the Helper's hands. *(image 19)*

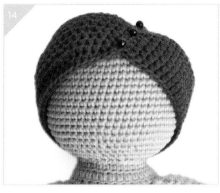

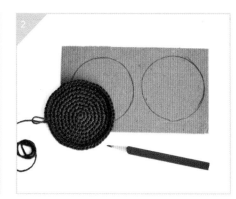

CAKE

Rounds 1-9: With **Color G**, repeat Rounds 1-9 of Granny Head.

Round 10: Working in **back loops** only, sc in each st around, changing to **Color A** in last st. (54 sc)

Round 11: With **Color A**, working in **back loops** only, sl st in each st around. (54 sl sts)

Round 12: Working in **back loops** only, sc in each st around. (54 sc)

Rounds 13-14: Sc in each st around. (54 sc)

At the end of Round 14, change to **Color H**.

Round 15: With **Color G**, working in **back loops** only, sl st in each st around. (54 sl sts)

Round 16: Working in **back loops** only, sc in each st around. (54 sc)

Note: *Two colors are used in Round 17. Color H is used only for the Bobbles. After using Color H, drop it to the inside and then pick it up when next needed, creating a strand on the inside. Keep the strands loose, so the Cake doesn't pull out of shape.*

Round 17: [With **Color G**, sc in each of next 5 sts, with **Color H**, bob in **front loop** only of next st] 9 times. (54 sts)

Round 18: Sc in each st around, changing to **Color A** in the last st. (54 sc)

Rounds 19-26: *(8 rounds)* repeat Rounds 11-18. (54 sc)

Round 27: With **Color A**, working in **back loops** only, sl st in each st around. (54 sl sts)

Round 28: Working in **back loops** only, sc in each st around. (54 sc)

Rounds 29-30: *(2 rounds)* Sc in each st around. (54 sc)

At the end of Round 30, change to **Color G**.

Round 31: Working in **front loops** only, r-sc in each st around. (54 sts) Fasten off and weave in ends.

Cake Edging Round: Working in unused front loops of Round 9, attach **Color B** in first st; r-sc in each st around. Fasten off and weave in ends.

CAKE BASE

Rounds 1-9: With **Color A**, repeat Rounds 1-9 of Cake. Fasten off, leaving a long tail for sewing.

CAKE PLATE

Rounds 1-9: Using **Color B**, repeat Rounds 1-9 of Cake.

At the end of Round 9, there are 54 sc.

Round 10: Sc in each of next 4 sts, inc in next st, [sc in each of next 8 sts, inc in next st] 5 times, sc in each of next 4 sts. (60 sc)

Round 11: [Sc in each of next 9 sts, inc in next st] 6 times. (66 sc)

Round 12: R-sc in each st around. (66 sts) Fasten off and weave in ends.

BERRIES

Raspberry (Make 3)

Round 1: With **Color H**, make a magic ring; 6 sc in ring. (6 sc) Tug tail to tighten ring. Do not join. Mark last st. Move marker at the end of each round.

Round 2: [Sc in next st, inc in next st] 3 times. (9 sc)

Round 3: Sc in each st around. (9 sc)

Round 4: Sc in each of next 8 sts, sl st in next st. (9 sts) Fasten off and weave in ends.

Blueberry (Make 3)

Round 1: With **Color E**, make a magic ring; 6 sc in ring. (6 sc) Tug tail to tighten ring. Do not join. Mark last st. Move marker at the end of each round.

Round 2: [Sc in next st, inc in next st] 3 times. (9 sc)

Round 3: Sc in each st around. (9 sc)

 - Stuff Blueberry lightly.

Round 4: [Dec, sc in next st] 3 times. (6 sc) Fasten off, leaving a tail for sewing.

 - Using yarn needle, weave the yarn tail through the front loops of each stitch and pull tight to close. Weave in all ends.

CAKE COILS (Make 6 - optional)

Wrap short strands of **Color F** tightly around a pencil. Use spray starch on them and leave them to dry. Repeat for each coil.

ASSEMBLY AND FINISHING TOUCHES
(use photos as guide)

Cake - Using the Cake Base as a template, cut out two circles of cardboard. Place one circle inside the Cake and add stuffing. Place the second circle on top of the stuffing. Using the long tail and yarn needle, sew the Cake Base to the Cake, matching stitches. *(image 1-9)*

Decorations - Arrange the Berries nicely on top of the Cake. Using a single strand of the berry color, sew in place. Randomly arrange the coils between the berries. *(image 10-11)*

Plate - Place the Cake onto the Plate, decorate with Cake coils (optional), and enjoy!

Little Bunny

design
Vivyane Veka
@happycrochetetc

Materials & Tools

HELLO Cotton Yarn
» **Main Color (MC):** Mocha (125)
» **Color A:** Cream (156) - for Sweater
» **Color B:** Baby Pink (101) - Facial Features & Bow

Hook Size
» 2.5 mm hook

Other
» Stitch Markers
» Yarn Needle
» Stuffing
» Safety Eyes - Round (12 mm) x 2
» Embroidery Needle
» Straight Pins

Finished Size
About 10″ (25 cm) tall

Skill Level
Easy

BUNNY

HEAD

Round 1: With **MC**, make a magic ring, 8 sc in ring. (8 sc) Tug tail to tighten ring. Do not join. Mark last st. Move marker at the end of each round.

Round 2: [Inc in next st] 8 times. (16 sc)

Round 3: [Sc in next st, inc in next st] 8 times. (24 sc)

Round 4: [Sc in each of next 2 sts, inc in next st] 8 times. (32 sc)

Round 5: Sc in next st, inc in next st, [sc in each of next 3 sts, inc in next st] 7 times, sc in each of next 2 sts. (40 sc)

Round 6: Sc in each st around. (40 sc)

Round 7: [Sc in each of next 4 sts, inc in next st] 8 times. (48 sc)

Round 8: Sc in each st around. (48 sc)

Round 9: [Sc in each of next 7 sts, inc in next st] 6 times. (54 sc)

Rounds 10-18: (9 rounds) Sc in each st around. (54 sc)

Round 19: [Sc in each of next 8 sts, inc in next st] 6 times. (60 sc)

Rounds 20-22: (3 rounds) Sc in each st around. (60 sc)

Round 23: [Sc in each of next 9 sts, inc in next st] 6 times. (66 sc)

Round 24: Sc in each st around. (66 sc)

Round 25: [Sc in each of next 9 sts, dec] 6 times. (60 sc)

Round 26: [Sc in each of next 8 sts, dec] 6 times. (54 sc)

Round 27: [Sc in each of next 7 sts, dec] 6 times. (48 sc)

- Insert Safety Eyes between Rounds 19 & 20, with 10 stitches between them.

- Start stuffing Head, adding more as you go.

Round 28: [Sc in each of next 4 sts, dec] 8 times. (40 sc)

Round 29: [Sc in each of next 3 sts, dec] 8 times. (32 sc)

Round 30: [Sc in each of next 2 sts, dec] 8 times. (24 sc)

Round 31: [Sc in each of next 2 sts, dec] 6 times. (18 sc)

Round 32: Working in **front loops** only, sc in each st around. (18 sc) Fasten off, leaving long tail for sewing.

- Finish stuffing Head firmly. (image 1)

BODY

Round 1: With **MC**, make a magic ring, 8 sc in ring. (8 sc) Tug tail to tighten ring. Do not join. Mark last st. Move marker at the end of each round.

Round 2: [Inc in next st] 8 times. (16 sc)

Round 3: [Sc in next st, inc in next st] 8 times. (24 sc)

Round 4: Sc in each st around. (24 sc)

Round 5: [Sc in next st, inc in next st] 12 times. (36 sc)

Round 6: Sc in each st around. (36 sc)

Round 7: [Sc in next st, inc in next st] 18 times. (54 sc)

Round 8: Sc in each st around. (54 sc)

Round 9: [Sc in each of next 8 sts, inc in next st] 6 times. (60 sc)

Round 10: Sc in each st around. (60 sc)

Round 11: [Sc in each of next 4 sts, inc in next st] 12 times. (72 sc)

Rounds 12-13: (2 rounds) Sc in each st around. (72 sc)

Round 14: [Sc in each of next 11 sts, inc in next st] 6 times. (78 sc)

Rounds 15-17: (3 rounds) Sc in each st around. (78 sc)

Round 18: [Sc in each of next 11 sts, dec] 6 times. (72 sc)

Rounds 19-20: (2 rounds) Sc in each st around. (72 sc)

Round 21: [Sc in each of next 10 sts, dec] 6 times. (66 sc)

Rounds 22-23: (2 rounds) Sc in each st around. (66 sc)

Round 24: [Sc in each of next 9 sts, dec] 6 times. (60 sc)

Round 25: Sc in each st around. (60 sc)

- Start stuffing Body, adding more as you go.

Round 26: [Sc in each of next 8 sts, dec] 6 times. (54 sc)

Round 27: Sc in each st around. (54 sc)

Round 28: [Sc in each of next 7 sts, dec] 6 times. (48 sc)

Round 29: Sc in each st around. (48 sc)

Round 30: [Sc in each of next 10 sts, dec] 4 times. (44 sc)

- Change to **Color A**, leaving a tail of about 47" (120 cm) on the outside of the Body. (image 2)

Round 31: Sc in each st around. (44 sc)

Round 32: Working in **back loops** only, [sc in each of next 9 sts, dec] 4 times. (40 sc) (image 3)

Round 33: Sc in each st around. (40 sc)

Round 34: [Sc in each of next 8 sts, dec] 4 times. (36 sc)

Round 35: Sc in each st around. (36 sc)

Round 36: [Sc in each of next 10 sts, dec] 3 times. (33 sc)

Round 37: Sc in each st around. (33 sc)

Round 38: [Sc in each of next 9 sts, dec] 3 times. (30 sc)

Round 39: Sc in each st around. (30 sc)

Round 40: [Sc in each of next 3 sts, dec] 6 times. (24 sc)

Round 41: Sc in each st around. (24 sc)

Round 42: [Sc in each of next 2 sts, dec] 6 times. (18 sc)

Fasten off, leaving a long tail for sewing to Head.

- Finish stuffing the Body.

- Using the long Color A tail, working in the front loops of Round 31, sc in each st around. (40 sc) Fasten off with a Needle Join and weave in ends. (image 4)

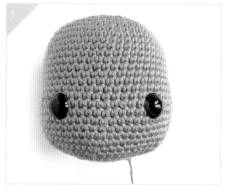
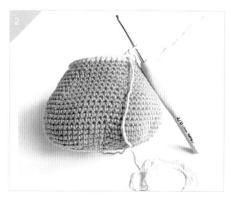

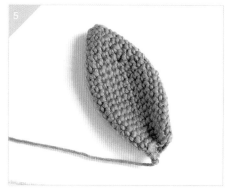

EAR (Make 2)

Note: The Ears are not stuffed.

Round 1: With **MC**, make a magic ring, 4 sc in ring. (4 sc) Tug tail to tighten ring. Do not join. Mark last st. Move marker at the end of each round.

Round 2: [Inc in next st] 4 times. (8 sc)

Round 3: Sc in each st around. (8 sc)

Round 4: [Sc in next st, inc in next st] 4 times. (12 sc)

Round 5: Sc in each st around. (12 sc)

Round 6: [Sc in each of next 2 sts, inc in next st] 4 times. (16 sc)

Round 7: Sc in each st around. (16 sc)

Round 8: [Sc in each of next 3 sts, inc in next st] 4 times. (20 sc)

Rounds 9-16: *(8 rounds)* Sc in each st around. (20 sc)

Round 17: [Sc in each of next 8 sts, dec] 2 times. (18 sc)

Round 18: Sc in each st around. (18 sc)

Round 19: [Sc in each of next 7 sts, dec] 2 times. (16 sc)

Round 20: Sc in each st around. (16 sc)

Round 21: [Sc in each of next 6 sts, dec] 2 times. (14 sc)

Round 22: Sc in each st around. (14 sc) Fasten off, leaving a long tail for sewing. *(image 5)*

ARM (Make 2)

Note: Only the Hands are stuffed.

Round 1: With **MC**, make a magic ring, 4 sc in ring. (4 sc)

Tug tail to tighten ring. Do not join. Mark last st. Move marker at the end of each round.

Round 2: [Inc in next st] 4 times. (8 sc)

Round 3: [Sc in next st, inc in next st] 4 times. (12 sc)

Rounds 4-6: *(3 rounds)* Sc in each st around. (12 sc) At the end of Round 6, change to **Color A** in last st, leaving a tail of about 16" (40 cm) on the outside of the Arm.

Round 7: Sc in each st around. (12 sc)

Round 8: Working in **back loops** only, sc in each st around. (12 sc)

Rounds 9-10: *(2 rounds)* Sc in each st around. (12 sc)

Round 11: [Sc in each of next 4 sts, dec] 2 times. (10 sc)

 - Stuff the Hands lightly.

Round 12: Dec, sc in each of next 3 sts, inc in next st, sc in each of next 4 sts. (10 sc)

Round 13: [Sc in each of next 3 sts, dec] 2 times. (8 sc)

Round 14: Dec, sc in each of next 3 sts, inc in next st, sc in each of next 2 sts. (8 sc)

Rounds 15-17: *(3 rounds)* Dec, sc in each of next 2 sts, inc in next st, sc in each of next 3 sts. (8 sc)

Last Row: Flatten Arm, working through both thicknesses, sc in each of next 4 sts. Fasten off, leaving a long tail for sewing.

 - Using the long Color A tail, working in the front loops of Round 7, sc in each st around. (12 sc) Fasten off with a Needle Join and weave in ends. *(image 6)*

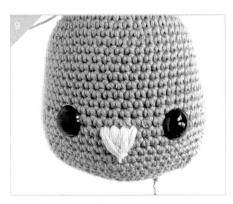
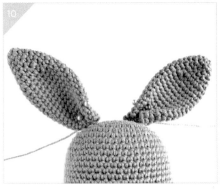

FOOT (Make 2)

Round 1: With **MC**, ch 5; sc in 2nd ch from hook, sc in each of next 2 ch, 2 sc in last ch; working on other side of starting chain, sc in each of next 3 ch. (8 sc) Do not join. Mark last st. Move marker at the end of each round.

Round 2: [Inc in next st, sc in each of next 2 sts, inc in next st] 2 times. (12 sc)

Round 3: Sc in each of next 2 sts, inc in next st, sc in next st, inc in each of next 4 sts, sc in next st, inc in next st, sc in each of next 2 sts. (18 sc)

Round 4: Sc in each of next 5 sts, inc in next st, sc in next st, inc in each of next 4 sts, sc in next st, inc in next st, sc in each of next 5 sts. (24 sc)

Round 5: Sc in each of next 10 sts, 2 hdc in each of next 4 sts, sc in each of next 10 sts. (28 sts)

- Sc in next st. Mark this sc as the new end of round. Move marker at the end of each round.

Round 6: Inc in next st, sc in each of next 10 sts, [2 hdc in next st, hdc in next st] 4 times, sc in each of next 8 sts, inc in next st. (34 sts)

Round 7: Sc in each of next 12 sts, hdc in next 10 sts, sc in each of next 12 sts. (34 sc)

Round 8: Sc in each of next 11 sts, [dec] 6 times, sc in each of next 11 sts. (28 sc)

Round 9: Dec, sl st in each of next 6 sts, [dec] 6 times, sl st in each of next 6 sts, dec. (20 sts) Fasten off, leaving a long tail for sewing.

- Stuff Foot firmly. *(image 7)*

COLLAR

Row 1: With **Color A**, ch 31; sc in 2nd ch from hook, hdc in next ch, dc in each of next 26 ch, hdc in next ch, sl st in last ch. Fasten off, leaving a long tail for sewing.

ASSEMBLY AND FINISHING

Nose - With **Color B**, embroider a triangle shape between the eyes, about 4 stitches across, over Rounds 20 to 22. *(image 8)*

Ears – Position the Ears on either side of the Head between Rounds 3 & 5 using straight pins. (You can position one vertically and the other one slightly inclined.) Using long tails, sew in place. *(image 9)*

Arms - Position the Arms on either side of the Body (slightly to the front) about 2 rounds below the Neck. Using long tails, sew in place. *(image 10)*

Feet - Position the Feet towards the front of the Body, so that the Bunny can sit unaided. Using long tails, sew in place. *(image 11)*

Body - Using the long tail, sew the Head to the Body, adding more stuffing to neck, if needed.

Collar - Wrap the Collar around the Neck and sew the each side together. Weave in all ends. With a strand of **Color B**, tie a small bow to the front of the Collar. *(image 12-13-14)*

Tail - With **Color A** yarn, make a small pompom and sew it to the back of the Body. It should help stabilize the Bunny. *(image 15)*

Cheeks and Eyebrows - With **Color B**, embroider the Cheeks close to the Eyes (over 1 round and 1 stitch wide) and embroider the Eyebrows 3 rounds above the outside corners of the Eyes (over 1 round and 1 stitch wide). *(image 16)*

Little Suzie

designer

Vivyane Veka

@happycrochetetc

Materials & Tools

HELLO Cotton Yarn

- » **Main Color (MC):** Cream (156)
- » **Color A:** Black (160) - for Hair
- » **Color B:** White (154) - for Skirt & Collar
- » **Color C:** Dark Yellow (120) - for Socks & Shirt
- » **Color D:** Bright Orange (118) - for Beret
- » **Color E:** Cherry Red (113) - for Shoes
- » **Color F:** Dark Brown (127) - for Face Embroidery

Hook Size

- » 2.0 mm hook

Other

- » Stitch Markers
- » Yarn Needle
- » Stuffing
- » Safety Eyes - Round (12 mm) x 2
- » Embroidery Needle
- » Straight Pins

Finished Size
About 8" (20 cm) tall

Skill Level
Intermediate

DOLL

HEAD & BODY

Head

Round 1: With **MC**, make a magic ring, 8 sc in ring. (8 sc) Tug tail to tighten ring. Do not join. Mark last st. Move marker at the end of each round.

Round 2: [Inc in next st] 8 times. (16 sc)

Round 3: [Sc in next st, inc in next st] 8 times. (24 sc)

Round 4: Sc in next st, inc in next st, [sc in each of next 2 sts, inc in next st] 7 times, sc in next st. (32 sc)

Round 5: [Sc in each of next 3 sts, inc in next st] 8 times. (40 sc)

Round 6: Sc in next st, inc in next st, [sc in each of next 4 sts, inc in next st] 7 times, sc in each of next 3 sts. (48 sc)

Round 7: [Sc in each of next 5 sts, inc in next st] 8 times. (56 sc)

Round 8: Sc in next each of next 3 sts, inc in next st, [sc in each of next 6 sts, inc in next st] 7 times, sc in each of next 3 sts. (64 sc)

Rounds 9-19: *(11 rounds)* Sc in each st around. (64 sc)

Round 20: [Sc in each of next 6 sts, dec] 8 times. (56 sc)

Round 21: Sc in next each of next 2 sts, dec, [sc in each of next 5 sts, dec] 7 times, sc in each of next 3 sts. (48 sc)

Round 22: [Sc in each of next 4 sts, dec] 8 times. (40 sc)

- Insert Safety Eyes on front of Head between Rounds 16 & 17, with 10 stitches between them. (The back of Head is where rounds begin and end.)

- Start stuffing Head, adding more as you go.

Round 23: Sc in next st, dec, [sc in each of next 3 sts, dec] 7 times, sc in each of next 2 sts. (32 sc)

Round 24: [Dec] 16 times. (16 sc)

Round 25: [Sc in each of next 2 sts, dec] 4 times. (12 sc)

Round 26: Working in **front loops** only, sc in each sc around, changing to **Color C** in last st. (12 sc) Fasten off **MC**. Continue with Body. *(image 1)*

- Stuff Head firmly.

Body

Round 1: With **Color C**, sc in each sc around. (12 sc)

Round 2: [Sc in next st, inc in next st] 6 times. (18 sc)

Round 3: [Sc in each of next 2 sts, inc in next st] 6 times. (24 sc)

Round 4: Sc in each st around. (24 sc)

Round 5: [Sc in each of next 3 sts, inc in next st] 6 times. (30 sc)

Rounds 6-7: *(2 rounds)* Sc in each st around. (30 sc)

Round 8: Sc in each of next 8 sts, inc in next st, sc in each of next 14 sts, inc in next st, sc in each of next 6 sts. (32 sc)

Rounds 9-11: *(3 rounds)* Sc in each st around. (32 sc)

Round 12: Working in **back loops** only, sc in each st around, changing to **Color B** in last st. (32 sc) Fasten off **Color C**.

Round 13: With **Color B,** working in **back loops** only, sc in each st around. (32 sc)

Rounds 14-15: *(2 rounds)* Sc in each st around. (32 sc) *(image 2)*

- Stuff the Body.

- Flatten the last round, marking the center 2 stitches at front and back, with 16 stitches on either side. *(image 3-4)*

- Work 2 more sc to end at side edge. Mark last sc as new beginning of round. Move marker each round.

Left Leg

Round 1: Sc in each of next 8 sc, skip next 16 sts, sc in each of next 8 sc, changing to **MC** in last st. (16 sc) *(image 5)*

Round 2: With **MC**, working in **back loops** only, [sc in each of next 2 sts, dec] 4 times. (12 sc)

- Stuff Body and Legs, adding more as you go.

Round 3: [Sc in each of next 4 sts, dec] 2 times. (10 sc)

Rounds 4-16: *(13 rounds)* Sc in each st around. (10 sc) At the end of Round 16, change to **Color C** in last st. Fasten off **MC**.

Round 17: With **Color C**, sc in each st around. (10 sc)

Round 18: Working in **back loops** only, sc in each st around. (10 sc) Continue with Foot.

Note: *The end of Round 18 should be on the inside of the Leg. (image 6)*

- Stuff the Leg.

Left Foot

Round 1: Sc in next st, inc in each of next 3 sts, sc in each of next 6 sts. (13 sc)

Round 2: Sc in each of next 3 sts, inc in next st, sc in next st, inc in next st, sc in each of next 7 sts. (15 sc)

Round 3: Sc in each sc around. (15 sc)

Round 4: [Sc in next st, dec] 5 times. (10 sc)

- Stuff the Foot.

Round 5: [Dec] 5 times. (5 sc) Fasten off, leaving a long tail.

- Using the long tail and yarn needle, close the opening, and weave in ends.

Right Leg

Round 1: Leaving a tail, attach **Color B** with sc to first skipped st on Round 15 of Body, sc in each of next 15 sc, changing to **MC** in last st. Mark last st. Move marker each round.

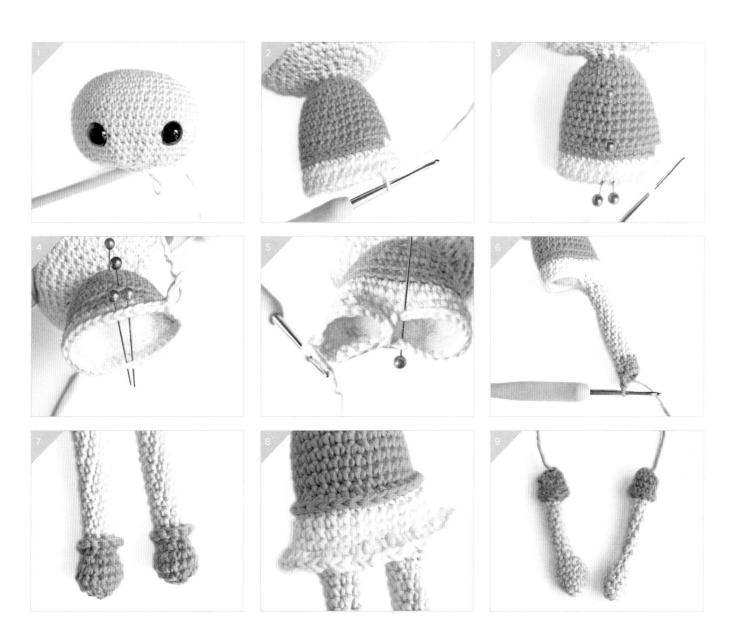

- Using the starting tail and yarn needle, sew the gap closed between the Legs.

Rounds 2-18: Repeat Rounds 2-18 of Left Leg.

Note: The end of Round 18 should be on the outside edge of the Leg.

 - Stuff the Leg.

Right Foot

Rounds 1-5: Repeat Rounds 1-5 of Left Foot.

 - Using the long tail and yarn needle, close the opening, and weave in ends.

Socks

Round 1: Holding Doll upside down, working in the unused front loops on Round 17 of Legs, attach **Color C** with sc to any st, [inc in next st, sc in each of next 2 sts] 3 times. (13 sc) Fasten off with Needle Join and weave in ends. *(image 7)*

 - Repeat on other Leg.

Skirt

Round 1: Holding Doll upside down, working in the unused front loops on Round 12 of Body, attach **Color B** with sc to any st, sc in each of next 31 sts. (32 sc) Do not join. Mark last st. Move marker at the end of each round.

Round 2: Sc in each st around. (32 sc)

Round 3: [Sc in each of next 7 sts, inc in next st] 4 times. (36 sc)

Rounds 4-5: *(2 rounds)* Sc in each st around. (36 sc)

Round 6: [Sc in next st, 2 dc in next st] around. (54 sts) Fasten off with Needle Join and weave in ends. *(image 8)*

T-Shirt Edging

Round 1: Holding Doll upside down, working in the unused front loops on Round 11 of Body, attach **Color C** with sc to any st, sc in each of next 31 sts. (32 sc) Fasten off with Needle Join and weave in ends. *(image 8)*

119

EAR (Make 2)

Row 1: With **MC**, ch 3, (hdc, 3 dc, hdc) in 3rd ch from hook. Fasten off, leaving a long tail for sewing.

ARM (Make 2)

Round 1: With **MC**, make a magic ring, 4 sc in ring. (4 sc) Tug tail to tighten ring. Do not join. Mark last st. Move marker at the end of each round.

Round 2: [Inc in next st] 4 times. (8 sc)

Round 3: [Sc in each of next 3 sts, inc in next st] 2 times. (10 sc)

Rounds 4-5: *(2 rounds)* Sc in each st around. (10 sc)

Round 6: [Sc in each of next 3 sts, dec] 2 times. (8 sc)

 - Stuff Hands lightly.

Round 7: [Sc in each of next 2 sts, dec] 2 times. (6 sc)

 - Start stuffing Arms, adding more as you go.

Rounds 8-15: *(8 rounds)* Sc in each st around. (6 sc) At the end of Round 15, change to **Color C** in last st.

Round 16: With **Color C**, [sc in next st, inc in next st] 3 times. (9 sc)

Round 17: Working in **back loops** only, sc in each st around. (9 sc)

Round 18: Sc in each st around. (9 sc) Fasten off, leaving a long tail.

 - Using the long tail and yarn needle, close the opening, leaving a tail for sewing.

Sleeve Edging

Round 1: Holding Arm upside down, working in the unused front loops on Round 16 of Arm, attach **Color C** with sc to first st, sc in each of next 8 sts. (9 sc) Fasten off with Needle Join and weave in ends.

- Repeat on other Arm. *(image 9)*

HAIR

Round 1: With **Color A**, make a magic ring, 8 sc in ring. (8 sc) Tug tail to tighten ring. Do not join. Mark last st. Move marker at the end of each round.

Rounds 2-14: Repeat Rounds 2-14 of Head.

Round 15: [Sc in each of next 15 sts, inc in next st] 4 times. (68 sc) Work continues in Rows.

Row 1: Sc in each of next 43 sts. (43 sc) Leave remaining stitches unworked.

Row 2: Ch 1, turn, dec *(using first 2 sts)*, sc in each of next 39 sts, dec *(using last 2 sts)*. (41 sc) *(image 10)* Leave remaining stitches unworked.

Rows 3-6: *(4 rows)* Ch 1, turn, sc in each st across. (41 sc)

Row 7: Ch 1, turn, inc in first st, sc in each of next 7 sts, dec, [sc in each of next 8 sts, dec] 2 times, sc in each of next 10 sts, inc in last st. (40 sc)

Row 8: Ch 1, turn, inc in first st, [sc in each of next 11 sts, dec] 2 times, sc in each of next 12 sts, inc in last st. (40 sc)

Row 9: Ch 1, turn, inc in first st, sc in each of next 38 sts, inc in last st. (42 sc)

Row 10: Ch 1, turn, sc in each st across. (42 sc)

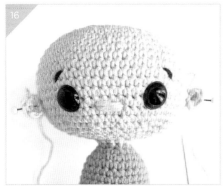

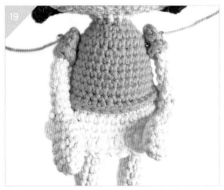

Row 11: Ch 1, turn, inc in first st, sc in each of next 40 sts, inc in last st. (44 sc) Fasten off, leaving a long tail for sewing. *(image 11)*

Hair Bangs

Row 1: With right side facing, working in remaining sts on Round 15 of Hair, attach **Color A**, to first st, sc in each st across. (25 sc)

Row 2: Ch 1, turn, inc in first st, sc in each of next 23 sts, inc in last st. (27 sc) Fasten off and weave in ends.

BERET

Rounds 1-8: With **Color D**, repeat Rounds 1-8 of Head.

Round 9: [Sc in each of next 7 sts, inc in next st] 8 times, (72 sc)

Round 10: [Sc in each of next 11 sts, inc in next st] 6 times. (78 sc)

Rounds 11-14: *(4 rounds)* Sc in each st around. (78 sc)

Round 15: [Sc in each of next 11 sts, dec] 6 times. (72 sc)

Round 16: [Sc in each of next 4 sts, dec] 12 times. (60 sc)

Round 17: Working in **front loops** only, [sc in each of next 3 sts, dec] 12 times. (48 sc) Fasten off using Needle Join and weave in all ends. *(image 12)*

Beret Stem

With **Color D**, ch 8, 2 dc in 4th ch from hook, hdc in next ch, sl st in each of next 3 ch. Fasten off, leaving long tail for sewing. *(image 13-14)*

SHOE (Make 2)

Round 1: With **Color E**, make a magic ring, 6 sc in ring. (6 sc) Tug tail to tighten ring. Do not join. Mark last st. Move marker at the end of each round.

Round 2: [Inc in next st] 6 times. (12 sc)

Round 3: [Sc in next st, inc in next st] 6 times. (18 sc)

Round 4: [Sc in each of next 2 sts, inc in next st] 6 times. (24 sc)

Round 5: Sc in each of next 8 sts, [dec] 4 times, sc in each of next 8 sts. (20 sc)

Round 6: Sc in each of next 8 sts, [dec] 2 times, sc in each of next 8 sts. (18 sc)

Round 7: Sc in each of next 6 sts. Leave remaining sts unworked.

Last Row: Ch 1, turn, sl st in each of next 12 sts, ch 6. Fasten off, leaving long tail for sewing straps to shoes. *(image 15)*

COLLAR

Row 1: With **Color B**, ch 21, starting in 2nd ch from hook, sc in each sc across. (20 sc)

Row 2: Ch 2, turn, 3 dc in first st, hdc in next st, sc in each of next 16 sts, hdc in next st, (3 dc, ch 2, sl st) in last st. (24 sts & 2 ch-2 lps) Fasten off, leaving long tail.

ASSEMBLY AND FINISHING

Nose - With **MC**, embroider a Nose between Rounds 17 and 18, between the Eyes, using straight stitches, about 4 stitches wide. *(image 16)*

Eyebrows - With **Color F**, embroider the Eyebrows 2 rounds above the outside corners of the Eyes (over 1 round and 2 stitches wide). *(image 16)*

Ears – Position the Ears on either side of the Head between Round 16 and 17, taking care that the Hair does not cover the Ears, and sew in place. *(image 16)*

Hair - Position the Hair on the Head and sew in place. *(image 17)*

Mouth - With **Color F**, embroider a small, smiling Mouth under the Nose (over 1 round and 2 stitches wide). *(image 18)*

Arms - Position the Arms on either side of the Body, 2 rounds below the Neck, and sew in place. *(image 19)*

Collar - Wrap the Collar around the Neck and sew both ends together, weaving in ends. With a small strand of **Color E**, thread through both sides of the Collar and tie together in front. *(image 20)*

Beret - Sew the Beret Stem to the top of the Beret. Position the Beret on Head, and sew in place (optional). *(image 21)*

Shoes - Place the Shoes on the Feet and sew the Straps to the first slip stitch on Last Row of the Shoes. *(image 22)* Weave in all ends.

Audrey

designer

Skaiste Kivci
@skaistekivci

Materials & Tools

HELLO Cotton Yarn

» **Main Color (MC):** Off-White (155) - for Body
» **Color A:** Brown (126) - for Hair
» **Color B:** Light Pink (102) - for Dress
» **Color C:** Beige (157) - for Dress
» **Color D:** Red (114) - for Shoes & Hat

Hook Size

» 2.5 mm hook

Other

» Stitch Markers
» Yarn Needle
» Stuffing
» Straight Pins
» DMC Embroidery Floss - Black (for Eyes)
» Embroidery Needle
» Cosmetic Blusher

Finished Size
About 12¼" (31 cm) tall

Skill Level
Intermediate

SPECIAL STITCHES & TECHNIQUES

Puff Stitch (puff): [Yarn over hook, insert hook in specified stitch and pull up a loop (to height of an hdc-stitch)] 4 times, yarn over and draw through all 9 loops on the hook.

PATTERN NOTES

1. The body parts of the doll are worked in spiral rounds.

2. Fill the body parts with stuffing as you go.

DOLL

BODY & HEAD

Shoe & Leg (Make 2)

Round 1: With **Color D**, make a magic ring, 6 sc in ring. (6 sc) Do not join. Mark last st. Move marker at the end of each round.

Round 2: Inc in each st around. (12 sc)

Rounds 3-8: *(6 rounds)* Sc in each st around. (12 sc)

Round 9: Working in **front loops** only, [sl st in next st, ch 2] 12 times, changing color to **MC** in last st. (24 sc) Continue with Leg. *(image 1)*

Leg

Round 1: With **MC**, working in unused **back loops** of Round 8, sc in each st around. (12 sc) *(image 2)*

Rounds 2-24: *(23 rounds)* Sc in each st around. (12 sc)

At the end of Round 24, for the First Leg, fasten off and weave in ends. For the Second Leg, do not fasten off. Continue with Body.

Body

Round 1: *(Joining Legs)* Ch 6, working on First Leg, sc in any st, sc in each of next 11 sc; working in ch-6, sc in each of next 6 ch; working on Second Leg, sc in each of next 12 sc; working on other side of ch-6, sc in each of next 6 ch. (36 sc) Mark last stitch. Move marker each round. *(image 3)*

Round 2: [Inc in next st, sc in each of next 10 sts, inc in next st, sc in each of next 6 sts] 2 times. (40 sc) *(image 4)*

Rounds 3-8: *(6 rounds)* Sc in each st around. (40 sc)

Round 9: Sc in each of next 6 sts, dec, [sc in each of next 8 sts, dec] 3 times, sc in each of next 2 sts. (36 sc)

Rounds 10-11: *(2 rounds)* Sc in each st around. (36 sc)

Round 12: Sc in each of next 6 sts, dec, [sc in each of next 7 sts, dec] 3 times, sc in next st. (32 sc)

Rounds 13-14: *(2 rounds)* Sc in each st around. (32 sc)

Round 15: [Sc in each of next 6 sts, dec] 4 times. (28 sc)

Rounds 16-17: *(2 rounds)* Sc in each st around. (28 sc)

Round 18: [Sc in each of next 5 sts, dec] 4 times. (24 sc)

Rounds 19-20: *(2 rounds)* Sc in each st around. (24 sc)

Round 21: [Sc in each of next 4 sts, dec] 4 times. (20 sc)

Rounds 22-23: *(2 rounds)* Sc in each st around. (20 sc)

Round 24: [Sc in each of next 3 sts, dec] 4 times. (16 sc)

Round 25: Sc in each st around. (16 sc)

Round 26: [Sc in each of next 2 sts, dec] 4 times. (12 sc)

Round 27: Sc in each st around. (12 sc) *(image 5)* Continue with Head.

Head

Round 1: [Inc in next st] 12 times. (24 sc)

Round 2: [Sc in each of next 3 sts, inc in next st] 6 times. (30 sc)

Round 3: [Sc in each of next 4 sts, inc in next st] 6 times. (36 sc)

Round 4: [Sc in each of next 5 sts, inc in next st] 6 times. (42 sc)

Round 5: [Sc in each of next 6 sts, inc in next st] 6 times. (48 sc)

Round 6: [Sc in each of next 7 sts, inc in next st] 6 times. (54 sc)

Round 7: [Sc in each of next 8 sts, inc in next st] 6 times. (60 sc) *(image 6-7)*

Rounds 8-19: *(12 rounds)* Sc in each st around. (60 sc)

Round 20: [Sc in each of next 8 sts, dec] 6 times. (54 sc)

Round 21: [Sc in each of next 7 sts, dec] 6 times. (48 sc)

Round 22: [Sc in each of next 6 sts, dec] 6 times. (42 sc)

Round 23: [Sc in each of next 5 sts, dec] 6 times. (36 sc)

Round 24: [Sc in each of next 4 sts, dec] 6 times. (30 sc)

Round 25: [Sc in each of next 3 sts, dec] 6 times. (24 sc)

Round 26: [Sc in each of next 2 sts, dec] 6 times. (18 sc)

Round 27: [Sc in next st, dec] 6 times. (12 sc)

Round 28: [Dec] 6 times. (6 sc) Fasten off, leaving a long tail.

 - Using long tail and yarn needle, close the opening. *(image 8)*

ARM (Make 2)

Round 1: With **MC**, make a magic ring, 6 sc in ring. (6 sc) Do not join. Mark last st. Move marker at the end of each round.

Round 2: [Sc in next st, inc in next st] 3 times. (9 sc)

Rounds 3-4: *(2 rounds)* Sc in each st around. (9 sc)

Round 5: Sc in each of next 3 sts, **puff** in next st *(thumb)*, sc in each of next 5 sts. (8 sc & 1 puff stitch)

Round 6: Sc in each st around. (9 sc)

Round 7: Sc in each of next 3 sts, inc in next st, sc in each of next 5 sts. (10 sc)

Rounds 8-27: *(20 rounds)* Sc in each st around. (10 sc)

 - Finish stuffing Arm.

Last Row: Flatten Arm, working through both thicknesses, sc in each of next 5 sts (5 sc) Fasten off, leaving a long tail for sewing.

- Position the Arms on either side of the Body between Rounds 58 & 59, with thumbs facing forward, and using long tail, sew in place.

HAIR

Round 1: With **Color A**, make a magic ring, 6 sc in ring. (6 sc) Tug tail to tighten ring. Do not join. Mark last st made. Move marker at the end of each round.

Round 2: Inc in each st around. (12 sc)

Round 3: [Sc in next st, inc in next st] 6 times. (18 sc)

Round 4: [Sc in each of next 2 sts, inc in next st] 6 times. (24 sc)

Round 5: [Sc in each of next 3 sts, inc in next st] 6 times. (30 sc)

Round 6: [Sc in each of next 4 sts, inc in next st] 6 times. (36 sc)

Round 7: [Sc in each of next 5 sts, inc in next st] 6 times. (42 sc)

Round 8: [Sc in each of next 6 sts, inc in next st] 6 times. (48 sc)

Round 9: [Sc in each of next 7 sts, inc in next st] 6 times. (54 sc)

Round 10: [Sc in each of next 8 sts, inc in next st] 6 times. (60 sc)

Rounds 11-22: *(12 rounds)* Sc in each st around. (60 sc) *(image 14)*

Round 23: Sl st in next st, [ch 35, starting in 2nd ch from hook, sc in each of next 34 ch; working on Rnd 22, sl st in next st] 35 times; sl st in each of next 6 sts, [ch 40, starting in 2ⁿᵈ ch from hook, sc in each of next 39 ch; working on Rnd 22, sl st in next st] 3 times; sl st in each of next 2 sts, [ch 45, starting in 2ⁿᵈ ch from hook, sc in each of next 44 ch; working on Rnd 22, sl st in next st] 3 times; sl st in each of next 10 sts. (35 strands of 34 sc, 3 strands of 39 sc, 3 strands of 44 sc, & 40 sl sts) Fasten off, leaving a long tail for sewing. *(image 15-18)*

- Position the Hair on the Head with the 6 longer strands to the front, a little to the side, and sew in place. *(image 19-20)*

- Make two braids using three long strands each, and sew to Head along hair-line.

from hook, sc in each of next 25 ch *(tie made)*, sl st in last sc made. Fasten off and weave in ends. *(image 21-22)*

- Place Hat on Doll's Head. If you want to, you can sew the Hat in place.

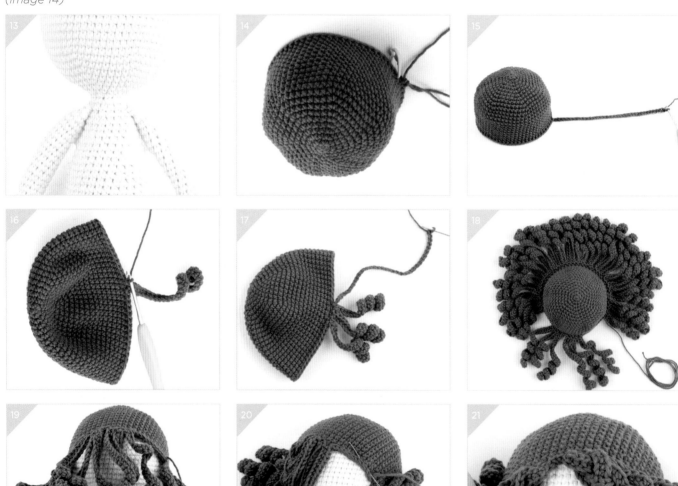

FINISHING THE DOLL

- Mark the position of the Eyes, and using Colour A by splitting the strands in two, embroider the Eyes and Eyelashes between Rounds 10 & 11 with 6 stitches between them.
  (image 23-28)

- With **MC**, embroider the Nose one round below the Eyes, using a few horizontal straight stitches over three stitches. *(image 29)*

- Apply some Blusher to the cheeks. *(image 30)*

DRESS

Yoke

Row 1: With **Color B**, ch 30, starting in 6th ch from hook, sc in each of next 24 ch. (24 sc)

Row 2: Ch 1, turn, sc in first st, sc in each of next 2 sts, inc in next st, [sc in each of next 3 sts, inc in next st] 5 times. (30 sc)

Row 3: Ch 1, turn, sc in first st, sc in each of next 3 sts, inc in next st, [sc in each of next 4 sts, inc in next st] 5 times. (36 sc)

Row 4: Ch 1, turn, sc in first st, sc in each of next 4 sts, inc in next st, [sc in each of next 5 sts, inc in next st] 5 times. (42 sc)

Row 5: Ch 1, turn, sc in first st, sc in each of next 6 sts, ch 6, skip next 7 sts *(armhole)*, sc in each of next 14 sts, ch 6, skip next 7 sts *(armhole)*, sc in each of next 7 sts. (28 sc & 2 ch-6 lps)

Row 6: Ch 1, turn, sc in first st, sc in each of next 6 sts; working in ch-6, sc in each of next 6 ch, sc in each of next 14 sts; working in ch-6, sc in each of next 6 ch, sc in each of next 7 sts. (40 sc)

Rows 7-10: *(4 rows)* Ch 1, turn, sc in each st across. (40 sc)

Row 11: Ch 1, turn, working in **back loops** only, sc in each sc across. Work continues in rounds.

Under Skirt

Round 1: Ch 1, turn, sc in each st around; join with sl st to first sc. (40 sc)

Round 2: Ch 2, 2 dc in each st around; join with sl st to first dc. (80 dc)

Rounds 3-12: *(10 rounds)* Ch 2, dc in each st around; join with sl st to first dc. (80 dc)

Round 13: Ch 2, (dc, ch 2, dc) in same st as joining, skip next st, [(dc, ch 2, dc) in next st, skip next 2 sts] around; join with sl st to first dc. (27 v-sts)

Round 14: Ch 1, sc in same st as joining, [4 dc in next ch-2 sp, skip next dc, sc in next dc] around, omitting last sc on final repeat; join with sl st to first sc. (27 sc & 27 groups of 4-dc) Fasten off and weave in ends.

Over Skirt

Round 1: Holding dress upside down, working in unused **front loops** on Round 10 of Yoke, attach **Color C** to any st at back of dress, ch 2, (dc, ch 1, dc) in each st around; join with sl st to first dc. (40 v-sts)

Rounds 2-11: Ch 2, (dc, ch 1, dc) in each ch-1 sp around; join with sl st to first dc. (40 v-sts)
At the end of Round 11, fasten off and weave in ends.

Sleeve

Round 1: Working around armhole, attach **Color B** in first skipped st, ch 1, work 2 sc in each stitch and row around armhole. (32 sc) Do not join. Mark last st. Move marker at the end of each round.

Rounds 2-4: *(3 rounds)* Sc in each st around. (32 sc)

Round 5: [Dec] 16 times, sl st in next st. Fasten off and weave in ends. Repeat Rounds 1-5 for other Sleeve.

 - Place finished Dress on Doll.

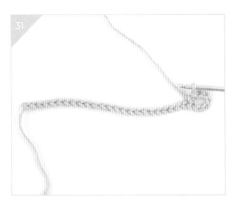

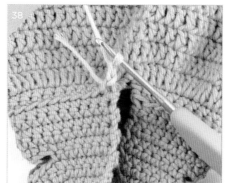

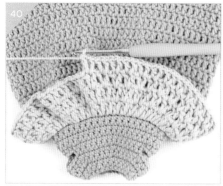

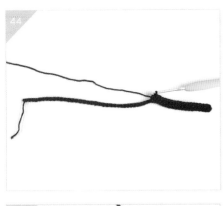  

HAT

Row 1: With **Color D**, ch 56, starting from 2nd ch from hook, hdc in each of next 55 ch. (55 hdc) *(image 44)*

Row 2-15: *(14 rows)* Ch 1, turn, hdc in each st across. (55 hdc) *(image 45)*

Row 16: Ch 1, turn, sl st in each of first 5 sts, hdc in each of next 45 sts, sl st in each of last 5 sts. (45 hdc & 10 sl sts)

Row 17: Ch 1, turn, sl st in each of first 5 sts, sc in each of next 3 sts, hdc in each of next 39 sts, sc in each of next 3 sts, sl st in each of last 5 sts. (55 sts) *(image 46)*

Row 18: Fold the Hat in half, working through both thicknesses across last row, sl st in each of next 27 sts. Fasten off and weave in ends. *(image 47)*

Hat Ties

Attach **Color D** to corner at Row 1, ch 26, starting in 2nd ch from hook, sc in each of next 25 ch *(tie made)*, working in sides of rows, evenly work 33 sc across to corner at other end of Row 1; ch 26, starting in 2nd ch.

riley
The Rag Doll

designer
Mei Li Lee
@amigurumei

Materials & Tools

HELLO Cotton Yarn

» **Main Color (MC):** Cream (156) - for Head & Hands
» **Color A:** Brown (126) - for Hair
» **Color B:** Off-White (155) - for Body & Legs
» **Color C:** Dusty Blue (145) - for Sling Bag
» **Color D:** Blue (148) - for Skirt
» **Color E:** Baby Pink (101) - for Cheeks
» **Color F:** Nectarine (115) - for Nose
» **Color G:** Cherry Red (113) - for Body & Pigtail ties
» **Color H:** Green (133) - for Legs
» **Color I:** Yellow (123) - for Shoes

Hook Size

» 2.5 mm hook

Other

» Stitch Markers
» Yarn Needle
» Stuffing
» DMC Embroidery Floss – Black
» Embroidery Needle
» Black sewing thread and needle
» Craft Glue

Optional

» Weighted Stuffing Beads (Poly-Pellets)
» Nylon Ankle Stockings (to hold Stuffing Beads)

Finished Size
About 8¼" (21 cm) tall

Skill Level
Intermediate

SPECIAL STITCHES & TECHNIQUES

Invisible Decrease (inv-dec): Insert hook under the front loop of each of the next 2 stitches. Yarn over and pull the yarn through these 2 front loops (2 loops remain on hook). Yarn over and draw through both loops on hook.

French Knot: Bring threaded needle up from the wrong to right side of piece at the position where you want the knot (#1). Wrap the yarn around the needle the required number of times and insert the needle back through the piece close to where it came out (almost is the same hole as #1). Gently pull the needle and yarn through the wrapped loops to form the knot.

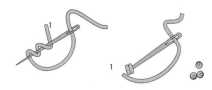

PATTERN NOTES

1. All parts are worked in spiral rounds, except for the Nose, Collar, & Skirt Straps.

DOLL

HEAD

Round 1: With **MC**, make a magic ring, 6 sc in ring. (6 sc)

Round 2: Inc in each st around. (12 sc)

Round 3: [Inc in next st, sc in next st] 6 times. (18 sc)

Round 4: [Inc in next st, sc in each of next 2 sts] 6 times. (24 sc)

Round 5: [Inc in next st, sc in each of next 3 sts] 6 times. (30 sc)

Round 6: [Inc in next st, sc in each of next 4 sts] 6 times. (36 sc)

Round 7: [Inc in next st, sc in each of next 5 sts] 6 times. (42 sc)

Round 8: [Inc in next st, sc in each of next 6 sts] 6 times. (48 sc)

Round 9: [Inc in next st, sc in each of next 7 sts] 6 times (54 sc)

Round 10: [Inc in next st, sc in each of next 8 sts] 6 times. (60 sc)

Round 11: [Inc in next st, sc in each of next 9 sts] 6 times. (66 sc)

Round 12: [Inc in next st, sc in each of next 10 sts] 6 times. (72 sc)

Round 13: [Inc in next st, sc in each of next 11 sts] 6 times. (78 sc)

Rounds 14-26: *(13 rounds)* Sc in each st around. (78 sc)

Round 27: [Inv-dec, sc in each of next 11 sts] 6 times. (72 sc)

Round 28: [Inv-dec, sc in each of next 10 sts] 6 times. (66 sc)

Round 29: [Inv-dec, sc in each of next 9 sts] 6 times. (60 sc)

Round 30: [Inv-dec, sc in each of next 8 sts] 6 times. (54 sc)

Round 31: [Inv-dec, sc in each of next 7 sts] 6 times. (48 sc)

Round 32: [Inv-dec, sc in each of next 6 sts] 6 times. (42 sc)

Round 33: [Inv-dec, sc in each of next 5 sts] 6 times. (36 sc)

Round 34: [Inv-dec, sc in each of next 4 sts] 6 times. (30 sc)

Round 35: [Inv-dec, sc in each of next 3 sts] 6 times. (24 sc)

Round 36: [Inv-dec, sc in each of next 2 sts] 6 times. (18 sc)

 - Start stuffing Head, adding more as you go.

Round 37: [Inv-dec, sc in next st] 6 times. (12 sc)

Round 38: [Inv-dec] 6 times. (6 sc) Fasten off, leaving a long tail.

 - Using yarn needle and tail, close the opening securely and weave in ends.

NOSE

Round 1: With **Color F**, ch 6, sl st in 2nd ch from hook, sc in the next ch, hdc in the next ch, dc in the next ch, 3 dc in last ch; working on other side of starting chain, dc in the next ch, hdc in the next ch, sc in the next ch, sl st in last ch. (11 sts) Fasten off with Needle Join, leaving a long tail for sewing.

CHEEK (Make 2)

Round 1: With **Color E**, make a magic ring, 6 sc in ring. (6 sc) Fasten off with Needle Join, leaving a long tail for sewing.

FINISHING THE FACE

Attaching the Nose

1. Position the Nose between Rounds 19 & 24, and sew in place.

Hint: Sewing the Nose onto the face first, helps where to position the Eyes and Mouth.

Eyes, Eyebrows & Mouth

1. Bring the Floss up from the underside of the Head, and embroider the closed Eyelids below Round 22, about 2 stitches away from the Nose, with a loose horizontal stitch about 4 stitches long. Make sure the floss is not pulled tight to give the eyelids a gentle, curved look.

2. Then embroider the Eyebrows from the top to the bottom of Round 17, positioned above each eye, with a diagonal backstitch 3 stitches long.

3. The Mouth is then embroidered below Round 25, centered underneath the Nose, with a loose horizontal backstitch 5 stitches long. When done, take the Floss out to the underside of the Head. *(image 1)*

4. Bring the black sewing thread up from the underside of the Head and embroider the Eyelashes with 3 vertical evenly spaced stitches along the Eyelids. When done, take the thread out to the underside of the Head. *(image 2)*

Hint: You may add some craft glue to form the mouth into a smile, using straight pins to hold the smile in place while the glue dries. (image 3)

5. Remember to knot all the floss and thread ends securely at the underside of the Head.

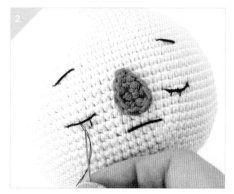
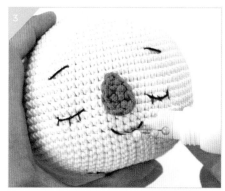

HAIR

Rounds 1-13: Using **Color A**, repeat Rounds 1-13 of Head.

Rounds 14-19: *(6 rounds)* Sc in each st around. (78 sc) Work continues in Rows.

Row 1: Ch 1, turn, sc in each of next 53 sts. (53 sc) Leave remaining sts unworked.

Rows 2-9: *(8 rows)* Ch 1, turn, sc in each st across. (53 sc)

Row 10: Ch 1, turn, sc in each of next 28 sts. (28 sc) Leave remaining sts unworked. Fasten off with Needle Join, leaving a long tail for sewing.

Pigtails (Make 2)

Round 1: With **Color G**, leaving a long tail, ch 7, sl st in first ch to form a ring; sc in each ch around, changing to **Color A** in last st. (6 sc)

Round 2: With **Color A**, sc in each st around. (6 sc)

Round 3: [Inc in next st, sc in next st] 3 times. (9 sc)

Round 4: [Inc in next st, sc in each of next 2 sts] 3 times. (12 sc)

Rounds 5-6: *(2 rounds)* Sc in each st around. (12 sc) At the end of Round 6, fasten off, leaving a long tail for sewing.

- Flatten each piece and using the long tail, whipstitch across the last round to close. Secure the yarn and trim any excess yarn.

ATTACHING HAIR

1. Position the Hair on the Head and sew in place using backstitches. *(image 4)*

2. Sew the Pigtails to each side of the Hair/Head, about 2 stitches from the side edge and about 2 rows from the bottom edge of the Hair.

Cheeks

1. Position and sew the Cheeks below each Eye. *(image 4)*

BODY

Rounds 1-10: Using **Color B**, repeat Rounds 1-10 of Head.

Rounds 11-15: *(5 rounds)* Sc in each st around. (60 sc) Change to **Color G**.

Rounds 16-17: *(2 rounds)* Sc in each st around. (60 sc) Change to **Color B**.

Rounds 18-19: *(2 rounds)* Sc in each st around. (60 sc) Change to **Color G**.

Rounds 20-21: *(2 rounds)* Sc in each st around. (60 sc) Change to **Color B**.

Rounds 22-23: *(2 rounds)* Sc in each st around. (60 sc) Change to **Color G**.

Round 24: [Inv-dec, sc in each of next 8 sts] 6 times. (54 sc)

Round 25: [Inv-dec, sc in each of next 7 sts] 6 times. (48 sc) Fasten off, leaving a long tail for sewing.

Skirt

Note: *For Round 1 only, the single crochet stitches are worked between the stitches below Round 15 of Body.*

(It doesn't matter whether you end up with more or less than 60 stitches, so long as you have worked all around the Body and joined the first round.)

Round 1: Holding the Body upside down, join **Color D** with a standing sc to any stitch below Round 15, sc in each stitch around; join with sl st to first sc. (60 sc) *(image 5-6)*

  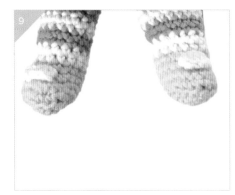

Round 2: [Inc in next st, sc in next st] 30 times. (90 sc) Do not join. Move marker at the end of each round. *(image 7)*

Rounds 3-10: *(8 rounds)* Sc in each st around. (90 sc) At the end of Round 10, fasten off and weave in ends. *(image 8)*

- Stuff body firmly. (Optional stuffing method: Place stuffing beads in a stocking and knot securely. Place the stuffed pouch in the base of Body, then add the regular stuffing.)

Skirt Straps

Front Straps (Make 2)

Row 1: With **Color D**, ch 12, starting in 2nd ch from hook, sc in each ch across. (11 sc) Fasten off, leaving a long tail for sewing.

Back Straps (Make 2)

Row 1: With **Color D**, ch 18, starting in 2nd ch from hook, sc in each ch across. (17 sc) Fasten off, leaving a long tail for sewing.

ARM (Make 2)

Round 1: With **MC**, make a magic ring, 5 sc in ring. (5 sc)

Round 2: Inc in each st around. (10 sc)

Rounds 3-4: *(2 rounds)* Sc in each st around. (10 sc) Change to **Color B**.

Rounds 5-6: *(2 rounds)* Sc in each st around. (10 sc) Change to **Color G**.

Rounds 7-8: *(2 rounds)* Sc in each st around. (10 sc) Change to **Color B**.

Rounds 9-10: *(2 rounds)* Sc in each st around. (10 sc) Change to **Color G**.

Rounds 11-12: *(2 rounds)* Sc in each st around. (10 sc) Change to **Color B**.

Rounds 13-14: *(2 rounds)* Sc in each st around. (10 sc) Change to **Color G**.

Rounds 15-16: *(2 rounds)* Sc in each st around. (10 sc) At the end of Round 16, fasten off, leaving a long tail for sewing.

- Stuff the Hand lightly – not the whole Arm.

LEG (Make 2)

Round 1: With **Color I**, make a magic ring, 6 sc in ring. (6 sc)

Round 2: Inc in each st around. (12 sc)

Round 3: [Inc in next st, sc in next st] 6 times. (18 sc)

Round 4: Working in **back loops** only, [inc in next st, sc in each of next 2 sts] 6 times. (24 sc)

Round 5: [Inv-dec] 3 times, sc in each of the next 18 sts. (21 sc)

Round 6: [Inv-dec] 3 times, sc in each of the next 15 sts. (18 sc)

Round 7: [Inv-dec] 3 times, sc in each of the next 5 sts, change to **Color B**, sc in each of the remaining 7 sts. (15 sc)

Round 8: Sc in each st around. (15 sc)

Round 9: Sc in each of the next 10 sts, change to **Color H**, sc in each of the next 5 sts. (15 sc)

Round 10: Sc in each st around. (15 sc)

Round 11: Sc in each of the next 10 sts, change to **Color B**, sc in each of the next 5 sts. (15 sc)

Round 12: Sc in each st around. (15 sc)

Round 13: Sc in each of the next 10 sts, change to **Color H**, sc in each of the next 5 sts. (15 sc)

Round 14: Sc in each st around. (15 sc)

Round 15: Sc in each of the next 10 sts, change to **Color B**, sc in each of the next 5 sts. (15 sc)

Round 16: Sc in each st around. (15 sc)

Round 17: Sc in each of the next 10 sts, change to **Color H**, sc in each of the next 5 sts. (15 sc)

Round 18: Sc in each of the next 10 sts only. (10 sc) Fasten off, leaving a long tail for sewing.

- Stuff the foot lightly - not the whole Leg.

SHOE "WINDOW" (Make 2)

Row 1: With **Color B**, ch 5, starting in 2nd ch from hook, sc in each ch across. (4 sc) Fasten off, leaving a long tail for sewing.

- Sew the "window" to the top part of the shoe.

(image 9)

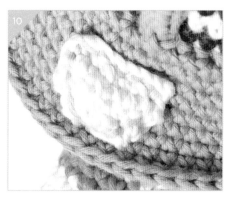

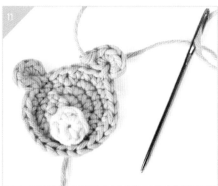

SKIRT POCKET

Row 1: With **Color B**, ch 7, starting in 2nd ch from hook, sc in each ch across. (6 sc)

Row 2: Ch 1, turn, sc in each st across. (6 sc)

Row 3: Ch 1, turn, dec, sc in each of the next 2 sts, dec. (4 sc)

Row 4: Ch 1, turn, [dec] twice. (2 sc) Fasten off, leaving a long tail for sewing.

- With **Color D**, embroider a border around the edges of the pocket using backstitches.

- Sew the Pocket to the front of the Skirt. *(image 10)*

SLING BAG

First Side

Round 1: With **Color C**, make a magic ring, 6 sc in ring. (6 sc)

Round 2: Inc in each st around. (12 sc)

Round 3: [Inc in next st, sc in next st] 6 times. (18 sc)

Round 4: [Inc in next st, sc in each of next 2 sts] 6 times. (24 sc) Fasten off, leaving a long tail for sewing.

Second Side

Rounds 1-4: Repeat Rounds 1-4 of First Side, but do not fasten off. Ch 50 *(or more if longer strap is needed)*, then fasten off, leaving a long tail for sewing.

Bear Ears (Make 2)

Round 1: With **Color C**, make a magic ring, 5 sc in ring. (5 sc) Fasten off, leaving a long tail for sewing.

- Sew the Ears to the First Side (without strap).

Bear Muzzle

Round 1: With **Color B**, make a magic ring, 6 sc in ring. (6 sc) Fasten off, leaving a long tail for sewing.

- Position the Muzzle on the First Side and sew in place. Knot all the ends at the back of the First Side. *(image 11)*

Finishing the Sling Bag

1. Using the Floss, embroider a Nose on the Muzzle with a French Knot (with 2 wraps around the needle) and embroider mouth and eyes with straight stitch and then With **Color E**, embroider the cheeks. *(image 12)*

2. With the First and Second Sides held together, whipstitch around. (If desired, leave the top open, like a real bag.) *(image 13)*

DOLL ASSEMBLY

1. Pin the pieces in position before sewing. *(image 14)*

2. Sew the Body to the finished Head, adding more stuffing before finishing.

3. Position the Arms and sew in place.

4. Flatten the tops of the Legs, and whipstitch them across Round 12 of Body, making sure the Doll can sit well.

5. Place the Sling Bag strap across the body of the Doll and, if needed, sew to secure it in place.

6. Sew front and back stripes in place with yarn tails. *(image 15)*

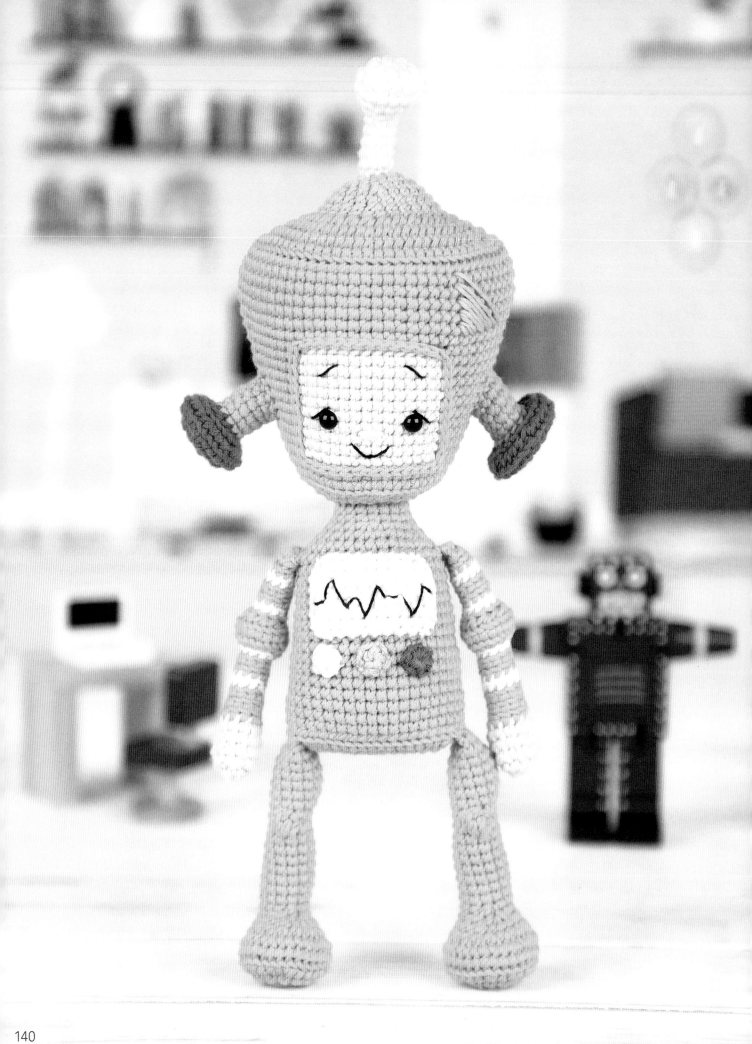

Robot Boy

designer

Gülizar Sezer

@amigurumibyguli

Materials & Tools

HELLO Cotton Yarn

» **Main Color (MC):** Beige (157) - for Face & Hands

» **Color A:** Mustard (124) - for Jumpsuit

» **Color B:** Sea Green (136) - for Head

» **Color C:** Brick Red (117) - for Ears

» **Color D:** Off-White (155) - for Arms & Screen

Hook Size

» 2.25 mm hook

Other

» Stitch Markers

» Yarn Needle

» Stuffing

» Safety Eyes - Black Round (6 mm) x 2

» DMC Embroidery Floss – Black & White – for facial & other features

» Embroidery Needle

Finished Size
About 11" (28 cm) tall

Skill Level
Advanced

SPECIAL STITCHES & TECHNIQUES

Single Crochet Decrease over 3 Stitches: (sc3tog):

[Insert hook in next stitch and pull up a loop] 3 times (4 loops on hook), yarn over and draw through all four loops. Decrease made.

HEAD

Round 1: With **Color B**, make a magic ring; ch 1, 9 sc in ring. (9 sc) Tug tail to tighten ring. Do not join. Mark last st. Move marker at the end of each round.

Round 2: Inc in each st around. (18 sc)

Round 3: [Sc in each of next 5 st, inc in next st] 3 times. (21 sc)

Round 4: [Sc in each of next 6 sts, inc in next st] 3 times. (24 sc)

Round 5 [Sc in each of next 7 sts, inc in next st] 3 times. (27 sc)

Round 6: [Sc in each of next 8 sts, inc in next st] 3 times. (30 sc) At the end of Round 6, change to **Color A**. Fasten off Color B.

Round 7: Inc in each st around. (60 sc)

Round 8: Sc in each of next 14 sts, inc in next st, sc in each of next 29 sts, inc in next st, sc in each of next 15 sts. (62 sc)

Round 9: Sc in each of next 13 sts, [inc in next st, sc in next st] 3 times, sc in each of next 24 sts, [sc in next st, inc in next st] 3 times, sc in each of next 13 sts. (68 sc)

Round 10: Sc in each of next 15 sts, inc in next st, sc in each of next 3 sts, inc in next st, sc in each of next 29 sts, inc in next st, sc in each of next 3 sts, inc in next st, sc in each of next 14 sts. (72 sc)

Round 11: Working in **back loops** only, sc in each st around. (72 sc)

Round 12: Sc in each of next 17 sts, dec, sc in each of next 34 sts, dec, sc in each of next 17 sts. (70 sc)

Round 13: Sc in each of next 16 sts, dec, sc in each of next 33 sts, dec, sc in each of next 17 sts. (68 sc)

Round 14: Sc in each of next 16 sts, dec, sc in each of next 32 sts, dec, sc in each of next 16 sts. (66 sc)

Round 15: Sc in each of next 15 sts, dec, sc in each of next 31 sts, dec, sc in each of next 16 sts. (64 sc)

Round 16: Sc in each of next 15 sts, dec, sc in each of next 30 sts, dec, sc in each of next 15 sts. (62 sc)

Round 17: Sc in each of next 14 sts, dec, sc in each of next 29 sts, dec, sc in each of next 15 sts. (60 sc)

Note: For Rounds 18-29, when changing colors, drop the "old" color to the inside and then pick it up again when needed, creating a strand on the inside. Keep the strands loose, so the Head doesn't pull out of shape.

Round 18: Sc in each of next 14 sts, dec, sc in each of next 7 sts; change to **MC** *(don't fasten off Color A)*, working in **back loops** only, sc in each of 14 sts; change to **Color A** *(don't fasten off MC)*, working in both loops, sc in each of next 7 sts, dec, sc in each of next 14 sts. (58 sc) *(image 1)*

Round 19: Sc in each of next 13 sts, dec, sc in each of next 7 sts; change to **MC**, sc in each of 14 sts; change to **Color A,** sc in each of next 6 sts, dec, sc in each of next 14 sts. (56 sc)

Round 20: Sc in each of next 21 sts; change to **MC**, sc in each of 14 sts; change to **Color A**, sc in each of next 21 sts. (56 sc)

Round 21: Sc in each of next 13 sts, dec, sc in each of next 6 sts; change to **MC**, sc in each of 14 sts; change to **Color A**, sc in each of next 6 sts, dec, sc in each of next 13 sts. (54 sc)

Round 22: Sc in each of next 12 sts, dec, sc in each of next 6 sts; change to **MC**, sc in each of 14 sts; change to **Color A**, sc in each of next 5 sts, dec, sc in each of next 13 sts. (52 sc)

Round 23: Sc in each of next 19 sts; change to **MC**, sc in each of 14 sts; change to **Color A,** sc in each of next 19 sts. (52 sc)

Round 24: Sc in each of next 12 sts, dec, sc in each of next 5 sts; change to **MC**, sc in each of 14 sts; change to **Color A,** sc in each of next 5 sts, dec, sc in each of next 12 sts. (50 sc)

Round 25: Sc in each of next 11 sts, dec, sc in each of next 5 sts; change to **MC**, sc in each of 14 sts; change to **Color A;** sc in each of next 4 sts, dec, sc in each of next 12 sts. (48 sc)

Round 26: Sc in each of next 17 sts; change to **MC**, sc in each of 14 sts; change to **Color A,** sc in each of next 17 sts. (48 sc)

Round 27: Sc in each of next 11 sts, dec, sc in each of next 4 sts; change to **MC**, sc in each of 14 sts; change to **Color A**, sc in each of next 4 sts, dec, sc in each of next 11 sts. (46 sc)

Round 28: Sc in each of next 10 sts, dec, sc in each of next 4 sts; change to **MC**, sc in each of 14 sts; change to **Color A**, sc in each of next 3 sts, dec, sc in each of next 11 sts. (44 sc)

Round 29: Sc in each of next 15 sts; change to **MC**, sc in each of 14 sts; change to **Color A**, sc in each of next 15 sts. (44 sc) Fasten off **MC**.

Round 30: Sc in each of next 10 sts, dec, sc in each of next 20 sts, dec, sc in each of next 10 sts. (42 sc) *(image 2)* *(image 3)*

- Insert Safety Eyes between Rounds 24 & 25, with 8 stitches between them.
- Stuff Head firmly to keep the shape, adding more as you go.

Round 31: Working in **back loops** only, [sc in each of next 5 sts, dec] 6 times. (36 sc)

Round 32: [Sc in each of next 2 sts, dec] 9 times (27 sc)

Round 33: [Sc in next st, dec] 9 times. (18 sc) Fasten off, leaving a long tail for sewing.

EAR (Make 2)

Note: *Ears are not stuffed.*

Round 1: With **Color C**, make a magic ring; ch 1, 12 sc in ring. (12 sc) Tug tail to tighten ring. Do not join. Mark last st. Move marker at the end of each round.

Round 2: Inc in each st around. (24 sc)

Round 3: [Sc in each of next 3 sts, inc in next st] 6 times. (30 sc)

Round 4: Working in **back loops** only, [sc in each of next 3 sts, dec] 6 times. (24 sc)

Round 5: Working in **back loops** only, [dec] 12 times, changing to **Color A** in last st. (12 sc) Fasten off **Color C**.

Round 6-10: *(5 Rounds)* Sc in each st around. (12 sc) Fasten off, leaving a long tail for sewing.

- Position the Ears on either side of the Head, between Rounds 22 & 26. Using long tails and yarn needle, sew them in place. *(image 4-5)*

ANTENNA

Round 1: With **Color D**, make a magic ring; ch 1, 9 sc in ring. (9 sc) Tug tail to tighten ring. Do not join. Mark last st. Move marker at the end of each round.

Round 2: Inc in each st around. (18 sc)

Rounds 3-4: *(2 Rounds)* Sc in each st around. (18 sc)

Round 5: [Sc in next st, dec] 6 times. (12 sc)

- Stuff Antenna lightly, adding more as you go.

Round 6: [Sc in next st, dec] 4 times. (8 sc)

Round 7-11: *(5 Rounds)* Sc in each st around. (8 sc) Fasten off, leaving a long tail for sewing.

- Position the Antenna on top of the Head. Using long tail and yarn needle, sew in place. *(image 6)*

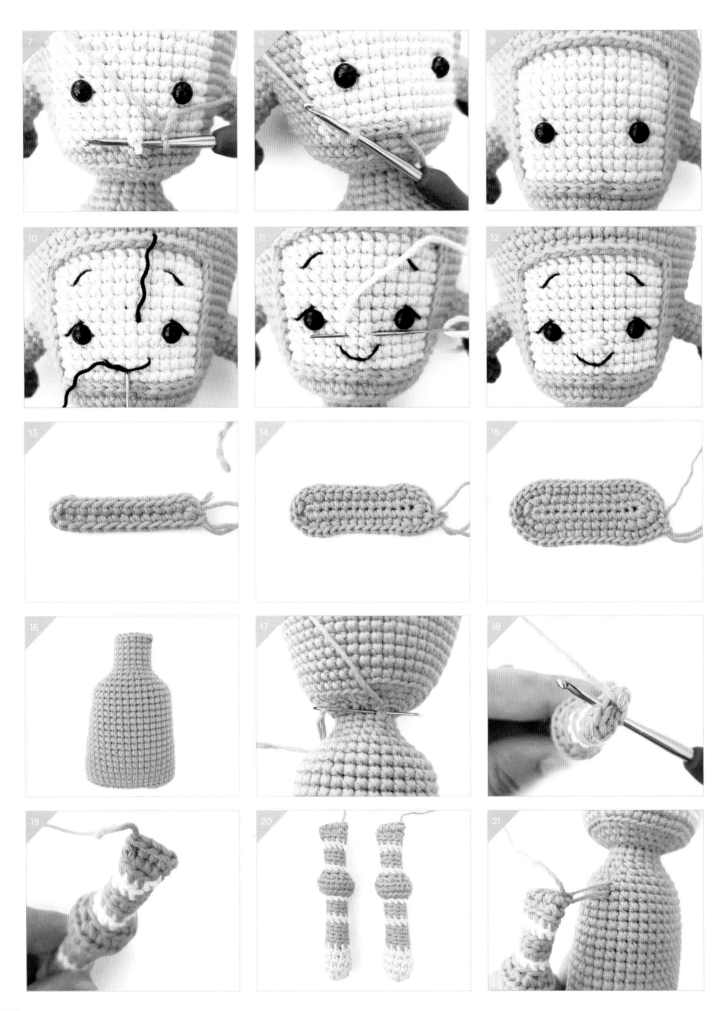

FINISHING THE FACE

1. Attach **Color A** to center stitch between Rounds 29 & 30 *(image 7)*, and slip stich between the stitches all around the Face (working in the unused front loops on Round 17 across the top). *(image 8-9)*

2. With Black Floss, embroider an Eyebrow about 4 rounds above each Eye, embroider an Eyelash on both Eyes, and embroider a Mouth – using a loose straight stitch and then shaping the Mouth with one small stitch. *(image 10)*

3. With MC, embroider a Nose using horizontal straight stitches. *(image 11-12)*

BODY

Round 1: With **Color A**, ch 13; inc in 2nd ch from hook, sc in each of next 10 ch, 4 sc in last ch, working on other side of starting chain, sc in each of next 10 ch, inc in last ch *(same ch as first in)*. (28 sc) *(image 13)* Do not join. Mark last st. Move marker at the end of each round.

Round 2: [Inc in each of next 3 sts, sc in each of next 8 sts, inc in each of next 3 sts] 2 times. (40 sc) *(image 14)*

Round 3: Inc in next st, sc in each of next 18 sts, inc in next st, sc in each of next 20 sts. (42 sc) *(image 15)*

Round 4: Inc in next st, sc in each of next 18 sts, inc in next st, sc in each of next 20 sts. (42 sc) *(image 15)*

Rounds 5-7: *(3 Rounds)* Sc in each st around. (42 sc)

Round 8: [Dec, sc in each of next 19 sts] 2 times. (40 sc)

Rounds 9-11: *(3 Rounds)* Sc in each st around. (40 sc)

Round 12: [Dec, sc in each of next 18 sts] 2 times. (38 sc)

Rounds 13-15: *(3 Rounds)* Sc in each st around. (38 sc)

Round 16: [Dec, sc in each of next 17 sts] 2 times. (36 sc)

Rounds 17-20: *(4 Rounds)* Sc in each st around. (36 sc)

Round 21: [Dec, sc in each of next 14 sts, dec] 2 times. (32 sc)

Round 22: *[Dec] 2 times, sc in each of next 8 sts, [dec] 2 times; repeat from * once more. (24 sc)

 - Stuff Body firmly to keep the shape, adding more as you go.

Round 23: [Dec, sc in each of next 3 sts] 2 times, [dec] 2 times, [sc in each of next 3 sts, dec] 2 times. (18 sc)

Rounds 24-29: *(6 Rounds)* Sc in each st around. (18 sc) Fasten off. *(image 16)*

 - Finish stuffing Body, adding more while sewing if necessary.

 - Using long tail and yarn needle, sew Head to Body, between Rounds 25 & 26. *(image 17)*

ARM (Make 2)

Round 1: With **MC**, make a magic ring; ch 1, 6 sc in ring. (6 sc) Tug tail to tighten ring. Do not join. Mark last st. Move marker at the end of each round.

Round 2: Inc in each st around. (12 sc)

Rounds 3-4: *(2 Rounds)* Sc in each st around. (12 sc)

Round 5: [Sc in each of next 4 sts, dec] 2 times, changing to **Color A** in last st. (10 sc) Fasten off **MC**.

Round 6: Sc in each st around. (10 sc)

Note: *Rounds 7-21 are all worked in* **back loops only.**

Rounds 7-8: *(2 Rounds)* Working in **back loops** only, sc in each st around. (10 sc)
At the end of Round 8, change to **Color D**. Don't fasten off **Color A**.

Round 9: Working in **back loops** only, sc in each st around, changing to **Color A** in last st. (10 sc) Don't fasten off **Color D**.

 - Start stuffing Arm firmly, adding more as you go.

Rounds 10-11: *(2 Rounds)* Working in **back loops** only, sc in each st around. (10 sc) At the end of Round 11, change to **Color D**. Don't fasten off **Color A**.

Round 12: Working in **back loops** only, sc in each st around, changing to **Color A** in last st. (10 sc) Don't fasten off **Color D**.

Round 13: Working in **back loops** only, inc in each st around. (20 sc)

Round 14: Working in **back loops** only, sc in each st around. (20 sc)

Round 15: Working in **back loops** only, [dec] 10 times, changing to **Color D** in last st. (10 sc) Don't fasten off **Color A**.

Round 16: Working in **back loops** only, sc in each st around, changing to **Color A** in last st. (10 sc) Don't fasten off **Color D**.

Rounds 17-18: *(2 Rounds)* Working in **back loops** only, sc in each st around. (10 sc) At the end of Round 18, change to **Color D**. Don't fasten off **Color A**.

Round 19: Working in **back loops** only, sc in each st around, changing to **Color A** in last st. (10 sc) Fasten off **Color D**.

Round 20: Working in **back loops** only, sc in each st around. (10 sc)

Round 21: Sc in each of next 3 sts, dec, sc in each of next 2 sts, dec. (7 sc) Leave remaining st unworked.

Last Row: Flatten Arm, working through both thicknesses, sc in each of next 4 sts. (4 sc) *(image 18)*

Fasten off, leaving a long tail for sewing. *(image 19-20)*

 - Position the Arms on either side of the Body, at about Round 20. Using long tails and yarn needle, sew them in place. *(image 21-22)*

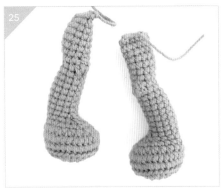

LEGS

Left Leg

Round 1: With **Color A**, make a magic ring; ch 1, 12 sc in ring. (12 sc) Tug tail to tighten ring. Do not join. Mark last st. Move marker at the end of each round.

Round 2: Inc in each st around. (24 sc)

Round 3: [Sc in each of next 3 sts, inc in next st] 6 times. (30 sc)

Round 4: Working in **back loops** only, sc in each st around. (30 sc)

Round 5: Sc in each st around. (30 sc)

Round 6: Sc in each of next 5 sts, [dec] 10 times, sc in each of next 5 sts. (20 sc)

Round 7: Dec, sc in each of next 7 sts, dec, sc in each of next 7 sts, dec. (17 sc)

 - Start stuffing Leg firmly, adding more as you go.

Round 8: Inc in next st, sc in each of next 4 sts, dec, **sc3tog**, dec, sc in each of 4 sts, inc in next st. (15 sc) *(image 23)*

Round 9: Sc in each of next 6 sts, sc3tog, sc in each of 6 sts. (13 sc)

Rounds 10-15: *(6 Rounds)* Sc in each st around. (13 sc)

Round 16: Dec, sc in each of next 9 sts, dec. (11 sc)

Round 17: Dec, sc in each of next 3 sts, 3 hdc in next stitch, sc in each of next 3 sts, dec. (11 sts)

Round 18: Inc in next st, sc in each of next 3 sts, sc3tog, sc in each of 3 sts, inc in next st. (11 sc)

Round 19: Inc in next st, sc in each of next 9 sts, inc in next st. (13 sc)

Rounds 20-24: *(5 Rounds)* Sc in each st around. (13 sc)

At the end of Round 24, make an extra decrease. (12 sc)

Last Row: Flatten Leg, working through both thicknesses, sc in each of next 6 sts. (6 sc) Fasten off, leaving a long tail for sewing. *(image 24)*.

Right Leg

Rounds 1-16: Repeat Rounds 1-16 of Left Leg.

Round 17: Dec, sc in each of next 4 sts, 3 hdc in next stitch, sc in each of next 2 sts, dec. (11 sts)

Rounds 18-24: Repeat Rounds 18-24 of Left Leg.

At the end of Round 24, make an extra decrease. (12 sc)

Last Row: Flatten Leg, working through both thicknesses, sc in each of next 6 sts. (6 sc) Fasten off, leaving a long tail for sewing. *(image 25)*.

 - Position the Legs on either side of the Body, at about Round 4. Using long tails and yarn needle, sew them in place. *(image 26-27)*

BUTTON
(Make 3 – 1 each with Color B, Color C, & Color D)

Round 1: With **Color**, make a magic ring; ch 1, 5 sc in ring. (5 sc) Tug tail to tighten ring. Fasten off with Needle Join, leaving a long tail for sewing.

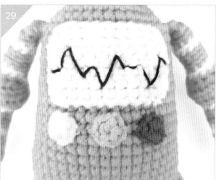

SCREEN

Row 1: With **Color D**, ch 10, starting in 2nd ch from hook, sc in each ch across. (9 sc)

Row 2-5: *(4 Rows)* Ch 1, turn, sc in each st across. (9 sc)

Edging Round: Ch 1, turn, sl st in each st and row around Screen; join with sl st to first sl st. Fasten off, leaving a long tail for sewing. *(image 28)*

- Position the Screen on front of the Body, between Rounds 13 & 20, and using long tails, sew in place.

- Position the Buttons below the Screen, between Rounds 10 & 12, and using long tails, sew in place.

- With Floss, embroider frequency lines on screen. *(image 29)*

- With **Color A**, embroider straight diagonal stitches across Rounds 12 & 18 of Head. *(image 30)*

harley
The Duckling

designer
Elisa Ems Domenig
@lululovesthemoon

Materials & Tools

HELLO Cotton Yarn

» **Color A:** Light Yellow (122) - for Body

» **Color B:** Orange (119) - for Beak & Legs

» **Color C:** Off-White (155) - Sweater & Eyes

» **Color D:** Robin's Egg Blue (151) - for Sweater

» **Color E:** Salmon (109) - for Cheeks

Hook Size

» 2.25 mm hook

Other

» Stitch Markers

» Yarn Needle

» Stuffing

» Safety Eyes - Black Round (8 mm) x 2

» DMC Embroidery Floss – Black (Eyes & Eyebrows)

» Embroidery Needle

Finished Size
About 6¼" (16 cm) tall

Skill Level
Easy

DUCKLING

HEAD

Round 1: With **Color A**, make a magic ring, 6 sc in ring. (6 sc) Do not join. Mark last st. Move marker at the end of each round.

Round 2: Inc in each sc around. (12 sc)

Round 3: [Sc in next sc, inc in next sc] around. (18 sc)

Round 4: [Sc in each of next 2 sc, inc in next sc] around. (24 sc)

Round 5: [Sc in each of next 3 sc, inc in next sc] around. (30 sc)

Round 6: [Sc in each of next 4 sc, inc in next sc] around. (36 sc)

Round 7: [Sc in each of next 5 sc, inc in next sc] around. (42 sc)

Round 8: Sc in each sc around. (42 sc)

Round 9: [Sc in each of next 6 sc, inc in next sc] around. (48 sc)

Round 10: Sc in each sc around. (48 sc)

Round 11: [Sc in each of next 7 sc, inc in next sc] around. (54 sc)

Rounds 12-14: *(3 rounds)* Sc in each sc around. (54 sc)

Round 15: [Sc in each of next 8 sc, inc in next sc] around. (60 sc)

Round 16: [Sc in each of next 9 sc, inc in next sc] around. (66 sc)

Round 17: [Sc in each of next 10 sc, inc in next sc] around. (72 sc)

Round 18: Sc in each sc around. (72 sc)

Round 19: [Sc in each of next 10 sc, dec] around. (66 sc)

Round 20: [Sc in each of next 9 sc, dec] around. (60 sc)

- Insert Safety Eyes between Rounds 17 & 18, with about 12 visible stitches between them.

Round 21: [Sc in each of next 8 sc, dec] around. (54 sc)

Round 22: [Sc in each of next 7 sc, dec] around. (48 sc)

Round 23: [Sc in each of next 6 sc, dec] around. (42 sc)

Round 24: [Sc in each of next 5 sc, dec] around. (36 sc)

Round 25: [Sc in each of next 4 sc, dec] around. (30 sc)

- Start stuffing Head firmly, adding more as you go.

Round 26: [Sc in each of next 3 sc, dec] around. (24 sc)

Round 27: [Sc in each of next 2 sc, dec] around. (18 sc)

Fasten off, leaving a long tail for sewing. Do not close the neck opening.

- Finish stuffing Head. *(image 1)*

FINISHING THE EYES

Eyes

- Using Black Floss, sculpt the Eyes by bringing the needle up through the base of the Head and out next to one Eye. Insert the needle on the opposite side of the Eye, bringing it out at the base of the Head. *(image 2)* Tuck the yarn under the Eye, while pulling tight on the yarn ends. *(image 3)* Tie the ends in a tight knot to secure. Repeat for the other Eye. *(image 4)*

  - With **Color C**, embroider a small stitch at the outer part of the Eye to create the highlight of the Eye. Repeat for the other Eye. *(image 5)*

Eyebrows

- Using Black Floss, embroider Eyebrows between Rounds 10 & 11 using small backstitches.

HEAD FEATHERS

Attach **Color A** with a slip stitch to the front of the Head between Rounds 4 & 5. [Ch 8, sl st in next st on Head] 3 times. (3 ch-8 lps) Fasten off and weave in ends. *(image 6)*

BEAK

Round 1: With **Color B,** ch 9; starting in 2nd ch from hook, sc in each of next 8 ch; working on other side of starting chain, sc in each of next 8 ch. (16 sc) Do not join. Mark last st. Move marker at the end of each round.

Rounds 2-5: *(4 rounds)* Sc in each sc around. (16 sc) Fasten off, leaving long tail for sewing..

- Position the Beak in a crescent shape to the center front of Head, between Rounds 17 & 19, and sew in place. *(image 6)*

CHEEK (Make 2)

Round 1: With **Color E,** make a magic ring, 7 sc in ring. (7 sc) Fasten off with Needle Join, leaving a long tail for sewing.

- Position the Cheeks on either side of the Face between Rounds 19 & 22, and sew in place. *(image 6)*.

BODY

Rounds 1-8: With **Color A,** repeat Rounds 1-8 of Head.

Rounds 9-12: Sc in each sc around. (42 sc)

At the end of Round 12, change to **Color D** in last stitch. Fasten off **Color A.**

Note: *For Rounds 13-18, do not fasten off when changing colors.*

Round 13: [Sc in each of next 5 sc, dec] around, changing to **Color C** in last st. (36 sc)

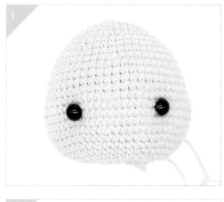

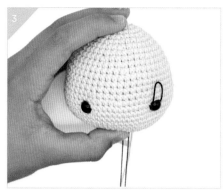
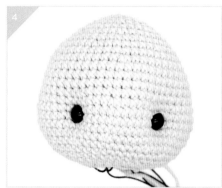

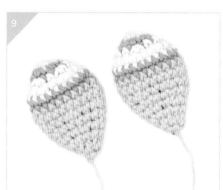

Round 14: Working in **back loops** only, sc in each sc around. (36 sc)

Round 15: Sc in each sc around, changing to **Color D** in last st. (36 sc)

Round 16: [Sc in each of next 4 sc, dec] around, changing to **Color C** in last st. (30 sc)

Round 17: Sc in each sc around. (30 sc)

Round 18: [Sc in each of next 3 sc, dec] around, changing to **Color D** in last st. (24 sc)

Round 19: Sc in each sc around, changing to **Color C** in last st. (24 sc) Fasten off **Color D.**

  - Start stuffing Body firmly, adding more as you go.

Round 20: [Sc in each of next 2 sc, dec] around. (18 sc)

Round 21: Sc in each sc around. (18 sc) Fasten off. Do not close the neck opening. *(image 7)*

  - Finish stuffing the Body.

  - Position the Head on the Body and sew in place, stuffing the neck firmly before finishing. *(image 8)*.

WING (Make 2)

Note: *Do not stuff Wings.*

Round 1: With **Color C**, make a magic ring, 5 sc in ring, changing to **Color D** in last st *(do not fasten off Color C)*. (5 sc) Do not join. Mark last st. Move marker at the end of each round.

Round 2: Inc in each sc around, changing to **Color C** in last st *(do not fasten off Color D)*. (10 sc)

Round 3: [Sc in next sc, inc in next sc] around. (15 sc)

Round 4: [Sc in each of next 2 sc, inc in next sc] around, changing to **Color D** in last st. (20 sc) Fasten off **Color C.**

Round 5: Sc in each sc around, changing to **Color A** in last st. (20 sc) Fasten off **Color D.**

Rounds 6-7: Sc in each sc around. (20 sc)

Round 8: [Sc in each of next 2 sc, dec] around. (15 sc)

Round 9: Sc in each sc around. (15 sc)

Round 10: [Sc in each of next sc, dec] around. (10 sc)

Round 11: Sc in each sc around. (10 sc)

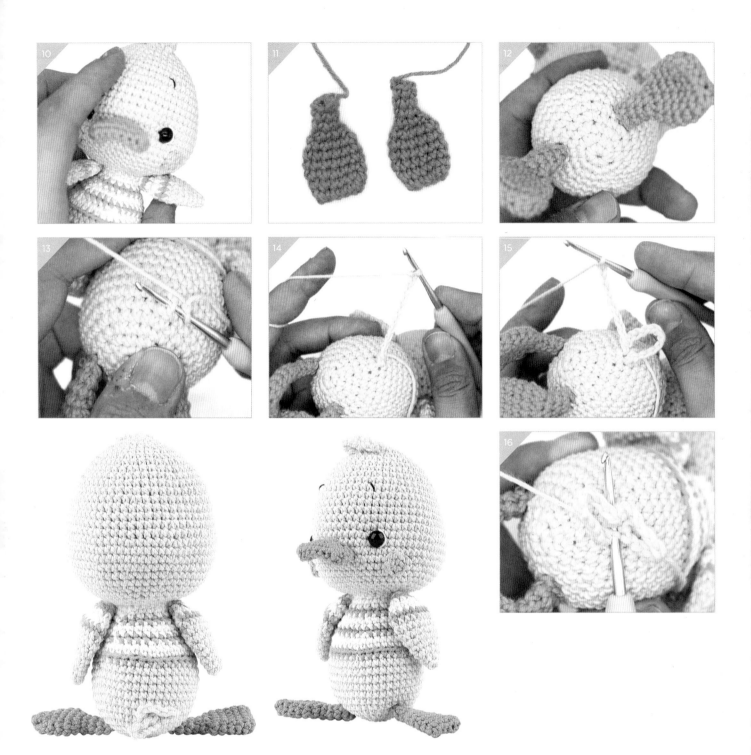

Round 12: [Dec] 5 times. (5 sc) Fasten off, leaving a long tail for sewing. *(image 9)*.

- Position Wings to either side of Body at Round 21, and sew in place. *(image 10)*.

LEG (Make 2)

Note: *Do not stuff Legs.*

Round 1: With **Color B,** ch 7; starting in 2nd ch from hook, sc in each of next 6 ch, working on other side of starting chain, sc in each of next 6 ch. (12 sc) Do not join. Mark last st. Move marker at the end of each round.

Rounds 2-6: Sc in each sc around. (12 sc)

Round 7: [Dec] 6 times. (6 sc)

Rounds 8-10: Sc in each sc around. (6sc)
At the end of Round 10, fasten off leaving a long tail for sewing. *(image 11)*.

- Position Legs towards the front of Body on Round 5, with about 8-9 stitches between them. Using long tails and yarn needle, sew in place. *(image 12)*

TAIL FEATHERS

Attach **Color A** with a slip stitch to center back between Rounds 6 & 7.

[Ch 10, sl st in same st] 2 times. (2 ch-10 lps) Fasten off and weave in ends. *(image 13 - image 16)*

Winter Bear

designer

Damla Savaş
@yesiltosba

Materials & Tools

HELLO Cotton Yarn

» **Main Color (MC):** Brown (126) - for Body

» **Color A:** Brick Red (117) - for Sweater

» **Color B:** Beige (157) - for Muzzle

» **Color C:** Black (160) - for Nose

» **Color D:** Apricot (110) - for Cheeks

» **Color E:** Sage (137) - for Hat

Hook Size

» 3.0 mm hook

Other

» Stitch Markers

» Yarn Needle

» Stuffing

» Safety Eyes - Black Round (6 mm) x 2

» DMC Embroidery Floss – Black & White – for facial & other features

» Embroidery Needle

Finished Size
About 11⅔" (30 cm) tall

Skill Level
Advanced

BEAR

BODY & HEAD

Round 1: With **MC**, make a magic ring, 6 sc in ring. (6 sc) Do not join. Mark last st. Move marker at the end of each round.

Round 2: Inc in each sc around. (12 sc)

Round 3: [Sc in next st, inc in next st] around. (18 sc)

Round 4: [Sc in each of next 2 sts, inc in next st] around. (24 sc)

Round 5: [Sc in each of next 3 sts, inc in next st] around. (30 sc)

Round 6: [Sc in each of next 4 sts, inc in next st] around. (36 sc)

Round 7: [Sc in each of next 5 sts, inc in next st] around. (42 sc)

Round 8: [Sc in each of next 6 sts, inc in next st] around. (48 sc)

Round 9: [Sc in each of next 7 sts, inc in next st] around. (54 sc)

Rounds 10-13: *(4 rounds)* Sc in each st around. (54 sc) At the end of Round 13, change to **Color A**. Fasten off MC.

Round 14: With **Color A**, working in **back loops** only, sc in each st around. (54 sc)

Round 15: Dec, sc in each of next 21 sts, dec, sc in each of next 29 sts. (52 sc)

Round 16: Dec, sc in each of next 20 sts, dec, sc in each of next 28 sts. (50 sc)

Round 17: Dec, sc in each of next 19 sts, dec, sc in each of next 27 sts. (48 sc)

Round 18: Dec, sc in each of next 18 sts, dec, sc in each of next 26 sts. (46 sc)

Round 19: Dec, sc in each of next 17 sts, dec, sc in each of next 25 sts. (44 sc)

Round 20: Dec, sc in each of next 16 sts, dec, sc in each of next 24 sts. (42 sc)

Round 21: Sc in each st around. (42 sc)

Round 22: Dec, sc in each of next 15 sts, dec, sc in each of next 23 sts. (40 sc)

Round 23: Sc in each st around. (40 sc)

Round 24: Dec, sc in each of next 14 sts, dec, sc in each of next 22 sts. (38 sc)

Round 25: Sc in each st around. (38 sc)

Round 26: Dec, sc in each of next 13 sts, dec, sc in each of next 21 sts. (36 sc)

Round 27: Sc in each st around. (36 sc)

Round 28: Dec, sc in each of next 12 sts, dec, sc in each of next 20 sts. (34 sc)

Round 29: Sc in each st around. (34 sc)

Round 30: Dec, sc in each of next 11 sts, dec, sc in each of next 19 sts. (32 sc)

Round 31: Sc in each st around. (32 sc)

Round 32: Working in **front loops** only, sc in each st around. (32 sc)

Round 33: [Sc in each of next 7 sts, inc in next st] 4 times. (36 sc)

Round 34: Sc in each st around. (36 sc)

Round 35: [Sc in each of next 8 sts, inc in next st] 4 times. (40 sc)

Rounds 36-37: Sc in each st around. (40 sc)
At the end of Round 37, fasten off with Needle Join and weave in ends. *(image 1 - image 3)*

Head

Round 1: Working in unused back loops of Round 31 of Body, attach **MC** to any stitch, sc in each st around. (32 sc) Do not join. Mark last st. Move marker at the end of each round. *(image 4)*

Round 2: [Sc in each of next 3 sts, inc in next st] 8 times. (40 sc)

Round 3: [Sc in each of next 3 sts, inc in next st] 10 times. (50 sc)

Round 4: [Sc in each of next 4 sts, inc in next st] 10 times. (60 sc)

Rounds 5-23: *(19 rounds)* Sc in each st around. (60 sc)

- Insert Safety Eyes between Rounds 11 & 12, about 12 stitches apart.
- Stuff the Body and Head, adding more as you go.

Round 24: [Sc in each of next 8 sts, dec] 6 times. (54 sc)

Round 25: [Sc in each of next 7 sts, dec] 6 times. (48 sc)

Round 26: [Sc in each of next 6 sts, dec] 6 times. (42 sc)

Round 27: [Sc in each of next 5 sts, dec] 6 times. (36 sc)

Round 28: [Sc in each of next 4 sts, dec] 6 times. (30 sc)

Round 29: [Sc in each of next 3 sts, dec] 6 times. (24 sc)

Round 30: [Sc in each of next 2 sts, dec] 6 times. (18 sc)

Round 31: [Sc in next st, dec] 6 times. (12 sc)

Round 32: [Dec] 6 times. (6 sc) Fasten off, leaving a long tail.

- Finish stuffing the Head.
- Using the long tail and yarn needle, close the opening.

MUZZLE

Round 1: With **Color B**, ch 8; 2 sc in 2nd ch from hook, sc in each of next 5 ch, 2 sc in last ch, working on other side of starting chain, sc in each of next 6 ch. (15 sc) Do not join. Mark last st. Move marker at the end of each round.

Round 2: Sl st in next st, sc in next st, hdc in each of next 2 sts, dc in next st, 2 dc in next st, hdc in next st, sl st in next st, hdc in next st, 2 dc in next st, dc in next st, hdc in each of next 2 sts, sc in each of next 2 sts. (17 sts)

Round 3: 2 sc in next st, sc in next st, sl st in each of next 4 sts, sc in next st, 2 hdc next st, hdc in each of next 2 sts, 2 hdc in next st, sc in next st, sl st in each of next 5 sts. (20 sts) Fasten off, leaving a long tail for sewing. *(image 5)*

CHEEK (Make 2)

Round 1: With **Color D**, make a magic ring, 6 sc in ring. (6 sc) Fasten off with Needle Join, leaving a long tail for sewing. *(image 6)*

FINISHING THE FACE

- With **Color C**, embroider the Nose and Freckles on the Muzzle, using the photos as a guide. *(image 7)*
- Position the Muzzle between the Eyes, and using the long tail, sew in place. *(image 8)*
- Position the Cheeks below the Eyes, and using the long tail, sew in place.
- With **MC** and yarn needle, insert the needle from the back of the neck and out next to one Eye. Insert the needle back through the Head and out at the back of neck. Tug the tails to create an eye socket. Knot the ends together. Repeat for other eye. *(image 9)*

ARM (Make 2)

Round 1: With **MC**, make a magic ring, 8 sc in ring. (6 sc) Do not join. Mark last st. Move marker at the end of each round.

Round 2: Inc in each sc around. (16 sc)

Round 3: [Sc in each of next 3 sts, inc in next st] 4 times. (20 sc)

Round 4: Sc in each st around. (20 sc)

Round 5: [Sc in each of next 8 sts, dec] 2 times. (18 sc)

Rounds 6-8: *(3 rounds)* Sc in each st around. (18 sc) At the end of Round 8, change to **Color A**.

Round 9: With **Color A**, working in **back loops** only, sc in each st around. (18 sc)

Rounds 10-23: *(14 rounds)* Sc in each st around. (18 sc)

- Stuff the Arm.

Round 24: [Sc in each of next 7 sts, dec] 2 times. (16 sc)

Last Row: Flatten Arm, working through both thicknesses, sc in each of next 7 sts, ch 5, sl st in first sc *(buttonhole)*. Fasten off, and weave in ends.

- Position the Buttons under the Neck and sew in place. Using the buttonhole, attach the Arms to the Buttons. *(image 10 - image 12)*

LEG (Make 2)

Round 1: With **MC**, make a magic ring, 6 sc in ring. (6 sc) Do not join. Mark last st. Move marker at the end of each round.

Round 2: Inc in each sc around. (12 sc)

Round 3: [Sc in next st, inc in next st] around. (18 sc)

Round 4: [Sc in each of next 2 sts, inc in next st] around. (24 sc)

Round 5: [Sc in each of next 3 sts, inc in next st] around. (30 sc)

Round 6: Working in **back loops** only, sc in each st around. (30 sc)

Rounds 7-9: *(3 rounds)* Sc in each st around. (30 sc)

- Start stuffing Leg, adding more as you go.

Round 10: [Sc in each of next 8 sts, dec] 3 times. (27 sc)

Round 11: Sc in each st around. (27 sc)

Round 12: [Sc in each of next 7 sts, dec] 3 times. (24 sc)

Rounds 13-22: *(10 rounds)* Sc in each st around. (24 sc)

Round 23: [Sc in each of next 4 sts, dec] 4 times. (20 sc)

Round 24: [Sc in each of next 3 sts, dec] 4 times. (16 sc)

Round 25: [Sc in each of next 2 sts, dec] 4 times. (12 sc)

Round 26: [Sc in next st, dec] 4 times. (8 sc)

 - Finish stuffing Leg.

Round 27: [Dec] 4 times. Fasten off, leaving a long tail.

 - Using the long tail and yarn needle, close the opening, leaving a tail for sewing.

 - Position the Legs on either side of the Body at Round 9, and sew in place. *(image 13 - image 16)*

HAT

Row 1: With **Color E**, ch 61, starting in 2nd ch from hook, dc in each ch across. (60 dc) Mark last st. Move marker at the end of each round.

Work continues in a spiral.

Round 2: Dc in first dc made on Rnd 1, [dc in next dc] around. (60 dc)

Rounds 3-11: Dc in each st around. (60 dc)

At the end of Round 11, fasten off leaving a long tail.

 - With **Color E**, make a big pompom.

 - Using long tail and yarn needle, weave through the stitches on the last round of Hat and gather tightly. Secure the yarn and using the same tail, sew on the pompom. Weave in ends.

 - Position Hat on Head and sew in place. *(image 17 - image 19)*

EAR (Make 2)

Round 1: With **MC**, make a magic ring, 6 sc in ring. (6 sc) Do not join. Mark last st. Move marker at the end of each round.

Round 2: Inc in each sc around. (12 sc)

Round 3: [Sc in next st, inc in next st] around. (18 sc)

Round 4: [Sc in each of next 2 sts, inc in next st] around. (24 sc)

Round 5: [Dec, sc in each of next 10 sts] 2 times. (22 sc)

Last Row: Flatten Ear, working through both thicknesses, sc in each of next 10 sts. Fasten off, leaving a long tail for sewing.

 - Position Ears on either side of Hat and sew in place.

 - Attach Eyeglasses to Face (optional). *(image 20-21)*

About the Designers

DAMLA SAVAŞ

@yesiltosba

Damla is known as "yesiltosba" on Instagram. After graduating in Physics at university, she worked in the field of occupational health and safety. When a close friend became pregnant, she decided to learn about crafting with yarn, as she wanted to make a gift for the new baby with her own hands. This is where Damla's amigurumi journey began! She lives in Ankara with her son and husband.

DİLEK BİRKAN

@dlkbrkn

Dilek is an avid amigurumi designer living in Istanbul with her husband, daughter, and cat. She learned to knit and crochet when she was about was six years old. After discovering amigurumi in 2014, she was hooked! Four years later, she started designing her own sweet amigurumi dolls and now sells her patterns in her Etsy shop, under the name "dlkbrkn".

ELISA EMS-DOMENIG

@lululovesthemoon

Elisa is a crochet artist and designer, living in a forest at the foot of the Austrian Alps with her husband, five children, and lots of farm animals. She finds her inspiration for the cute woodland toys while taking long walks through the forest with her two youngest children. Her beautiful designs and creations can be seen on her Instagram page, "Lulu loves the Moon". These timeless, heirloom treasures make long-term cuddle friends for children.

GÜLİZAR SEZER

@amigurumibyguli

Gülizar is a prolific amigurumi designer and the person behind "amigurumibyguli" on Instagram. In 2016, her amigurumi journey began, and not long after that she fell in love with designing cute animal toys and dolls. The patterns for her exceptional designs are for sale in her Etsy shop. Gülizar lives with her husband and two cats in Kütahya, Turkey.

KATE AND DASHA

@grannyscrochethook

Dasha and Kate, are real-life sisters from Saint Petersburg. They both have higher technical education, but never really got to practice their professions. As youngsters, they enjoyed crafting, drawing and cooking, but they only started crocheting recently because it then became trendy. They tried a lot of different crochet techniques, but amigurumi was the skill that took hold. Kate and Dasha originally started their Instagram account so that they could follow interesting artsy and crafty people - to learn from them and have fun. Despite the word "granny", used on their social media, they did not have any relatives to teach them the crafts. You can see their lovely designs on their Instagram account.

MEI LI LEE

@amigurumei

Mei, or better known as "Amigurumei", is a self-professed daydreamer who came across amigurumi quite by chance. Now she enjoys sharing the joy of the craft with like-minded daydreamers, splitting her hours between being a mom of three boys while designing lovely dolls. Each of her toys is packed with a little unique personality all of their own (much like her boys). The former journalist and craft columnist is also the author of Hello Kitty Crochet. She lives with her husband and boys in Malaysia.

SANDRA MULLER

@luciennecompotine

Sandra, who is known as "LucienneCompotine", is a Fine Arts graduate and textile designer based in France. Her passion for beautiful fabrics and colors is evident in her gorgeous creations. Her delightful dolls, with their own clothing and accessories, have a great place in her collections.

After starting out with knitting (to clothe her children), she found crochet and the world of amigurumi. Using tutorials and online videos to learn, she was soon inspired. Not long after that, her first little design was born. Since then, not a day goes by without her using her hook!

Today she shares this passion by displaying her work on her Instagram account and selling her designs in her Etsy shop. She lives with her husband and children in Lyon.

SKAISTĖ KIVCI

@skaistekivci

Skaistė is a translator and amigurumi designer based in Lithuania. She has been into handicrafts ever since she was a child. She happened to get into the charming, colourful world of amigurumi simply because she wanted to bring joy to her kids and friends by making them handmade toys. She feels lucky that she found this hobby, which also introduced her to like-minded peers and friends. She is a mom of three and lives in Lithuania with her family.

VIVYANE VEKA

@happycrochetetc

Vivyane, the amigurumi designer behind "Happy Crochet Etc..", is based in France. She fell into the crochet cauldron in December 2013. Up to then, she had been drawing and painting a lot, but was looking for a new activity that would re-boost her creativity and give it a new momentum. That is when she discovered the world of amigurumi - and it was exactly what she was looking for! Vivyane is a self-taught crocheter who learned through books and videos. It did not take her long to decide that she wanted to create her own designs. Today she collaborates with various craft brands and crochet magazines.